GO»
AHEAD

REALSCHULE BAYERN

Schulaufgabentrainer
für Schülerinnen und Schüler

Mit Lösungen und Lerntipps

8

Deine Audios findest du auf www.scook.de.
Dort gibst du den unten stehenden Zugangscode in die Box ein.

Dein Zugangscode auf www.scook.de | **cb9ux-hwjq8**

Cornelsen

GO»
AHEAD
REALSCHULE BAYERN

Go Ahead · Band 8
Schulaufgabentrainer mit Lösungen und Lerntipps

Erarbeitet von	Rebecca Kaplan, Mauer
Redaktion	Ursula Fleischhauer, Hannover Rebekka Gerlach (Lizenzmanagement) Klaus Unger (Projektleitung)
Bildquellen	**Titelbild** Shutterstock.com/Maridav (Läufer); Shutterstock.com/Andrey Bayda (Brooklyn Bridge, New York City) **Illustrationen** **Cornelsen/Christian Bartz** (S. 13, 21, 32, 35, 36) **Abbildungen** **S. 5/1:** Shutterstock.com/Mangostar, **/2:** Shutterstock.com/oneinchpunch, **/3:** Shutterstock.com/greenbluedream, **/4:** Shutterstock.com/Takanori Kudo, **/5:** Shutterstock.com/Elnur, **/6:** Shutterstock.com/Adam Calaitzis, **/Thumbnail Noelle:** Shutterstock.com/Stanley Jin; **S. 7:** Shutterstock.com/Mia2you; **S. 11/1:** Shutterstock.com/LouieLea, **/2:** Shutterstock.com/rj lerich, **/3:** Shutterstock.com/Will Hughes, **/Thumbnail Noelle:** Shutterstock.com/Stanley Jin; **S. 12:** Shutterstock.com/Becky Starsmore; **S. 17:** Shutterstock.com/nicostock; **S. 20:** Shutterstock.com/Syda Productions; **S. 22/Leiste:** Cornelsen/Corngreen Agentur GmbH; **S. 26/1:** Shutterstock.com/Bogdan Denysyuk, **/2:** Shutterstock.com/Fred Cardoso, **/3:** Shutterstock.com/Jordan Scanlan, **/4:** Shutterstock.com/Gorlov Alexander, **/5:** Shutterstock.com/lapandr, **/6:** Shutterstock.com/LanKS; **S. 29:** Shutterstock.com/LeDarArt; **S. 31:** Shutterstock.com/NatalieJean; **S. 34:** Shutterstock.com/Abu hasim.A; **S. 38:** Bridgeman Images/Auto: 1915 Ford Model T.; **S. 40:** Shutterstock.com/exsilentroot; **S. 41:** interfoto e.k./Hollywood Collection; **S. 43:** Shutterstock.com/Creative Photo Corner; **S. 45/li.:** Shutterstock.com/Sabina Dimitriu, **/2. v. li.:** Shutterstock.com/Timof, **/2. v. re.:** Shutterstock.com/MustafaNC, **/re.:** Shutterstock.com/Eric Von Seggern; **S. 50:** Shutterstock.com/Monkey Business Images; **S. 53:** Shutterstock.com/aceshot1; **S. 56/1 Thumbnails:** Shutterstock.com/chuhastock, **/2 Karte:** Shutterstock.com/ataur0002bd, **/3 Dollar:** Cornelsen/zweiband.media; **/4 Icons:** Shutterstock.com/art of 2 pixxels, **/ Diagramme:** Cornelsen/zweiband.media; **Statistik 1–5:** Statistics Canada, Frontier Counts; Visitor Travel Survey (preliminary); **Statistik 6:** Statistics Canada, CANSIM table 4270004 and Travel Between Canada and Other Countries; **Statistik 7:** Language Highlight Tables, 2016 Census; **S. 61:** Shutterstock.com/Microstocker.Pro; **S. 62:** Shutterstock.com/Adwo
Tonaufnahmen	Studio: Clarity Studio Berlin Regie und Aufnahmeleitung: Susanne Kreutzer Tontechnik: Gislinde Böhringer, Hüseyin Dönertas
Sprecherinnen und Sprecher	Sprecherinnen und Sprecher: Harley Aussoleil, Kristen Bush, Mala Ghedia, Jeffrey Mittleman, Darren Smith, Joshua Spriggs, Clare Wigfall, Ian Wood
Gestaltung und Technische Umsetzung	zweiband media, Berlin
Umschlaggestaltung	Verlag GmbH, Berlin, unter Verwendung der Entwürfe von hawemannundmosch, Berlin

www.cornelsen.de

1. Auflage, 2. Druck 2021

Druck: Athesiadruck GmbH

ISBN 978-3-06-35235-7

Inhalt

Lösungen und **Lerntipps** sowie die **Trackliste** und **Notentabellen** sind in der Mitte des Heftes eingeheftet.

Vorwort

Liebe Schülerin, lieber Schüler,

mit dem **Schulaufgabentrainer Go Ahead 8** kannst du dich gezielt auf deine Schulaufgaben in der Jahrgangsstufe 8 vorbereiten. Du findest hier zu den Units 1–5 in deinem Englischbuch jeweils zwei Schulaufgaben zum Üben. Die meisten Arbeitsanweisungen sind auf Englisch. Viele kennst du bereits aus deinem Schülerbuch. Manche enthalten Wörter, die du vielleicht noch nicht aktiv gelernt hast, die du aber im Dictionary deines Schülerbuches nachschlagen kannst. Einige weitere findest du auf Deutsch auf S. 29 im Lösungsteil.

In den Schulaufgaben gibt es manchmal **Lerntipps**, die dir bei der Bearbeitung der Aufgabe weiterhelfen.

Alle **Höraufnahmen** für die *Listening*-Aufgaben findest du online. Wenn es mehrere Teilaufgaben zu einem Hörtext gibt, kannst du dir zur Bearbeitung jeder Teilaufgabe die Aufnahme erneut anhören. Wenn du den Text lesen möchtest, findest du ihn abgedruckt im **Lösungsteil** in der Mitte deines Schulaufgabentrainers.

Am Anfang jeder Schulaufgabe steht die **Gesamtpunktzahl**, die du bei der richtigen Lösung aller Aufgaben erreichen kannst. Neben jeder Einzelaufgabe steht die Punktanzahl, die du für diese Aufgabe erhalten kannst. Für jede richtige Lösung in einem Satz und für jeden Satz beim *Guided writing* steht dir ein Punkt zu.

Wenn du alle Aufgaben in einer Schulaufgabe gelöst hast, überprüfe deine Antworten mit den Lösungen und Lösungsvorschlägen (*Guided writing*) im **Lösungsteil** in der Mitte des Heftes. Wenn du dich nicht selbst in die Versuchung bringen willst, vorzeitig in die Lösungen zu schauen, kannst du den **Lösungsteil** auch herausnehmen und an einem anderen Ort ablegen. Trage dann die Punktzahl, die du erreicht hast, in die leeren Kästchen ein und zähle alle Punkte zusammen. Sieh sie dir genau an, wenn du eine Aufgabe nicht korrekt gelöst hast, und mache die Aufgabe dann noch einmal.

Zur Notenbestimmung findest du auf S. 31 des **Lösungsteils** einen Schlüssel.

Wir wünschen dir viel Spaß beim Üben und viel Erfolg bei den Schulaufgaben!

The American dream

Schulaufgabe A

Unit 1

Gesamtpunktzahl _____ / 87   Note _____

1 READING Noelle's New York City posts   _____ / 8

Read Noelle's social media posts from New York City. Then complete the tasks.

1

eyeonnoelle

eyeonnoelle We're in New York!!! Our hotel is on West 40th Street, between 7th and 8th Avenues: near Macy's AND Times Square! Our room is small, but clean and quiet (for New York). I don't think we'll be spending a lot of time here, though: too much to see!

2

eyeonnoelle

eyeonnoelle After we had checked in and put our bags in our room, we went to Times Square. It's just like in the movies: thousands of people, lights (even in the day!), traffic, noise, street artists performing, stores … just amazing!

3

eyeonnoelle

eyeonnoelle One of my favorite stores in Times Square is all about my favorite candy: my friends know which one! They have every color of the rainbow and more: three floors of it! My family had a lot of trouble getting me out of there!

4

eyeonnoelle

eyeonnoelle Of course, we also had to look at some souvenirs. I have no idea what to bring back for my friends, but I'm sure I'll find something cool. How do you like all of these Statues of Liberty?!?

5

eyeonnoelle

eyeonnoelle Broadway!!! I can't believe I'm here! I love the theater and especially musicals and there are so many of them! You can buy cheap tickets in Times Square, so I think we'll go to a few shows while we're in the city. We got tickets for one of the plays that I really wanted to see: I can't wait!

6

eyeonnoelle

eyeonnoelle Waiting outside the theater to meet the stars! Maybe I can even get a selfie with my favorite actor! I'll definitely post that photo, so check my story again today!

1 Why doesn't it matter that Noelle's hotel room is small?

____

2 What are two things that Noelle likes about her hotel?

____

3 What did Noelle's family do before going to Times Square?

____

4 Where had Noelle already seen Times Square?

____

5 What does the picture in post number three show?

____

6 Why did Noelle post photo number 4?

____

7 What does photo number 5 symbolize for Noelle?

____

8 What does Noelle hope one of her next posts will show?

____

USE OF ENGLISH

2 LANGUAGE Writing the date

01

____ / 6

Listen and write the date in American English.

1	
2	
3	
4	
5	
6	

LERNTIPP

American English:
Du schreibst:
September 18, 2025
Du sagst:
September eighteenth, two thousand twenty-five

3 LANGUAGE The Statue of Liberty

____/18

a Fill in the gaps with the correct words to make questions. There are three words that you don't need. ____/9

are · can · did · has · have · how · what · when · where · who · why · will

1 ________ gave the Statue of Liberty to the United States?

2 ________ do you have to do before you go into the statue?

3 ________ does the statue stand?

4 ________ you already booked tickets?

5 ________ you go up to the statue's crown? *(happened in the past)*

6 ________ many steps are in the statue?

7 ________ did France give the statue to the U.S.? *(the reason)*

8 ________ you going to use the audio guide?

9 ________ was the statue opened to visitors for the first time? *(the year)*

b Match the number of each question from **a** with the correct answer below. There are three answers you don't need. ____/9

1 As a symbol of friendship. ☐

2 By boat. ☐

3 France. ☐

4 Get your bags checked. ☐

5 In 1886. ☐

6 At night. ☐

7 Yes, I did. ☐

8 354. ☐

9 In New York Harbor. ☐

10 No, I haven't. ☐

11 Yes, I am. ☐

12 No, she isn't. ☐

LERNTIPP

Die Lösung dieser und ähnlicher Aufgaben fällt dir leichter, wenn du zu jeder Frage die passende Antwort suchst, statt die Antworten den Fragen zuzuordnen. Das spart Zeit und Mühe, da es nicht zu jeder Antwort eine passende Frage gibt (drei Antworten bleiben ja übrig). So musst du z. B. bei den *Yes-/No-*Fragen nur bei den *Yes-/No-*Antworten diejenige mit dem passenden Verb aussuchen. Wenn eine Zahl gefragt ist, musst du bei den Antworten nur nach Zahlen schauen, usw.

4 WORDS Volunteering at a shelter

___/7

Use the word given in capitals at the end of some lines to form a word from the same word family that fits in the space on the same line.

I help out at a shelter for the __________ every	HOME
Saturday in my __________ . Usually I help to give	NEIGHBOR
food to families. A lot of them lost their apartments because	
they got sick and didn't have __________ . They had	INSURE
to pay for doctors' bills and couldn't afford the	
__________ . It isn't easy for kids living in a shelter:	RENT
it's often __________ and there are a lot of	NOISE
__________ rules. I'm always friendly and try to have	STRICTLY
fun with the little kids: working with them is a big	
__________ .	RESPONSIBLE

5 WORDS Around the city

___/7

Match the statements with the things they're talking about. There are three words you don't need.

1 ☐ "We can get off at Columbus Circle."

2 ☐ "They love sitting out there on warm summer nights, talking with their neighbors."

3 ☐ "There are five of them, but most people think of Manhattan when they think about New York City."

4 ☐ "I work at one of the big banks there."

5 ☐ "Which one do I take to get to Coney Island?"

6 ☐ "It's not just noisy: it's dangerous and bad for the environment."

7 ☐ "We went to the most amazing restaurant on 7th."

A traffic
B financial center
C brownstone
D avenue
E borough
F stoop
G store
H route
I skyscraper
J subway

6 SKILLS Filling in a form ____/12

Noelle had to fill in a travel application for the USA. Write the **numbers** from the information in each bubble in the right place on the form. You do not have to fill all spaces, and some information may go in more than one space.

ENTER INFORMATION Please give all answers in English.
Required fields are shown by an asterisk*.

APPLICANT / PASSPORT INFORMATION
Refer to your passport and enter all information in the same format.

Family Name* ____ First Name* ____

Gender* ◉ Male ◉ Female

Date of Birth* ____ City of Birth* ____

Country of Birth* ____ Passport Number* ____

Country of Citizenship* ____ National Identification Number ____

Issue Date* ____ Issuing Country* ____

Personal Identification Number ____ Expiration Date* ____

YOUR CONTACT INFORMATION
Please enter your contact information below.

Address Line 1* ____

Address Line 2 ____

Apartment Number ____ City* ____

State/Province/Region* ____ Country* ____

Telephone Type* ____ Country Code + Phone* ____

Email Address* ____

SOCIAL MEDIA (Optional)
Please enter information about your online activity.

Provider / Platform ____

Social Media Identity ____

CONTACT INFORMATION
WHILE IN THE U.S.

Name* ____

Address Line 1* ____

Address Line 2 ____

Apartment Number ____

City* ____

State* ____

Phone* Number ____

EMERGENCY CONTACT INFORMATION IN OR OUT OF THE U.S.
(family member or friend)

Family Name* ____ First (Given) Name* ____

Email Address* ____ Telephone* ____

QUESTIONS
1 Do you have a physical or mental illness?*
Are you a drug user or addict?*
Do you have a disease?* ____
2 Have you ever committed a crime that resulted in serious harm to property or another person?*

esta.cbp.dhs.gov

1 She was born on August 8, 2009.

2 Germany

3 She uses Instagram.

4 She was born and still lives in Munich.

5 She got her passport on March 14, 2020.

6 She lives at Elchweg 7.

7 If there's a problem, call her mother, Lili.

8 She'll be staying in Clifton, New Jersey.

9 She'll need to get a new passport in 2030.

10 Noelle is very healthy.

11 Noelle

12 She's putting her cell phone number on the form.

7 **MEDIATION** **A taxi ride in New York City** ____/ 14

Your mother speaks French every day at work but hasn't spoken English for years. You've just arrived at the airport in New York for your holiday. Your mum is hoping to improve her English here, but is still feeling too shy to speak with the taxi driver on the way to the hotel. It's your job to help her communicate with the taxi driver.

Driver: How are you doing this morning?

You: ____ (1 P)

Driver: Not too bad, thanks! Where to?

You: Mama, ____ (1 P)

Mother: Oh, wie hieß es nochmal? Ich muss mal schauen … sorry, hätte ich vorher machen sollen. Moment mal …

You: ____ (2 P)

Mother: Jetzt habe ich es … The Bryant Inn at Bryant Park.

You: ____ (1 P)

Driver: There's a lot of traffic this morning, so it'll take almost an hour.

You: ____ (2 P)

Mother: Und wie viel kostet es?

You: ____ (1 P)

Driver: Taxis from JFK airport to Manhattan always cost $52.

You: ____ (1 P)

Mother: Danke. Ich schließe mal so lange die Augen. Ich bin ganz müde!

Driver: Is your mother OK?

You: ____ (1 P)

Driver: So, here we are: The Bryant Inn.

You: Mama, ____ (1 P)

Mother: In Amerika gibt man mehr Trinkgeld als in Deutschland, also geben wir ihm 60 Dollar. Sag ihm, es stimmt so.

You: ____ (2 P)

Driver: Thanks. Have a good day.

You: ____ (1 P)

8 GUIDED WRITING A day in the Bronx

____/ 15

Noelle's second day in New York City was also great! Write captions (about 35 words each) to go along with her photos on these social media posts. Her notes will help you. You can also look at her posts from task 1 on page 5.

Photo1: subway · Bronx · zoo · little kids · favorite animal
Photo 2: late lunch · famous deli · friendly waitress · great coffee · big tip
Photo 3: evening · baseball game · big stadium · masses of people · NY won

Make sure to write:

- how you got there,
- what three places you went to and what you did in each place,
- how you liked each place or what was good/not so good.

1

eyeonnoelle

eyeonnoelle ______________________

2

eyeonnoelle

eyeonnoelle ______________________

3

eyeonnoelle

eyeonnoelle ______________________

Unit 1

The American dream

Schulaufgabe B

Gesamtpunktzahl ____ / 75 Note ____

1 LISTENING Shopping trip ____ / 14

02

Shreya is shopping for makeup at Macy's. Listen to her conversation and then complete the tasks.

a Number the events in the right order. ____ / 6

- ☐ Carlos offers to demonstrate some products.
- ☐ Shreya asks for directions to something in the store.
- ☐ Shreya describes a color she would like to try.
- ☐ Carlos introduces himself.
- ☐ Shreya criticizes something.
- ☐ Carlos describes how he got his job.

LERNTIPP

Die Informationen im Hörtext werden manchmal etwas anders ausgedrückt als in den dazugehörigen Aufgaben. Schau nach Synonymen und Umschreibungen für Wörter und Aussagen aus dem Hörtext.

b Complete the sentences. ____ / 8

1 Shreya is interested in FeatureFace makeup because she … ____________________ . (1 P)

2 Carlos has been working at FeatureFace for … ____________________ . (1 P)

3 To get the job, Carlos … ____________________ (1 P) and ____________________ . (1 P)

4 Cyber Cyan mixes … ____________________ and ____________________ . (1 P)

5 The light bulbs are so strong because it's better for … ____________________ . (1 P)

6 Shreya only buys … ____________________ . (1 P)

7 Shreya asks for directions to … ____________________ . (1 P)

USE OF ENGLISH

2 LANGUAGE Questions about a hotel ____ / 6

A group of friends is checking into a hotel. Ask questions about the underlined part of each answer.

1 ______________________________ Ali booked this hotel.

2 ______________________________ The elevator on the left goes to our floor.

3 ______________________________ The rooms on the west side have the best view.

4 ______________________________ The name of the hotel is on the key card.

5 ______________________________ Sam is paying the bill.

6 ______________________________ The vending machine is making that noise.

3 WORDS Deli customers ____ / 8

These customers eat breakfast in the same deli every day. One of the waitresses is describing them to a new waiter. Use the right forms of the words and phrases in the box to complete their profiles. There are four that you don't need.

addict · (to) appreciate · bagel · bill · coffee · cream cheese · deli · egg · gallon · mustard · nickname · state of mind · (to) tip

1

______________ ______________

2

Loves ______________

3

In no ______________ ______________ to make a decision

4

Usually doesn't ______________

5

Really hates ______________

6

Puts ______________ on everything

7

Never has enough money for the ______________

8

______________ : Big Mouth

4 **WORDS** **Good news!** ____/12

Fill in the missing words in Diego's diary entry. Make sure to use American English words and spelling, as well as the correct form of each word.

Today was a great day! My ____________ *(a short form of "mother")* found an ____________ *(a set of rooms for living in)* we can afford in our old ____________ *(an area of a town or city)*! It's clean, no ____________ *(a large brown insect that lives in buildings, especially if they are not clean)* … and best of all, it's not a ____________ *(a building where people without a home can stay)*! We can take all of our ____________ *(the things that you own)* over there next week and move in. It'll be great not to be ____________ *(without a place to live)* any more. No ____________ *(a time at which sb. must be home in the evening)*, no horrible living ____________ *(the situation in which people live, work or do things)*, no sharing a ____________ *(a room in which there is a toilet and water to wash yourself)* with strangers! My sister and I will have to share a bedroom, but it has two ____________ *(a small room in a larger room; you can put clothes and other things in it)*. I'm really looking forward to leaving this place! I think everything is going to be ____________ ____________ *(OK)* now.

5 **SKILLS** **Another way to say it** ____/8

You want the following things but can't remember the English words for them, so you paraphrase them. Use all of the words in the box in your explanations.

book · (to) buy · (to) call · country · drink · face · good · hairstyle · home · hot dog · lamp · photo · prettier · sauce · spicy · tea

1 mustard ____________

2 light bulb ____________

3 passport ____________

____

4 gel ____________

5 mobile phone ____________

6 makeup ____________

7 coffee ____________

8 deli ____________

6 **MEDIATION** **Information about visiting Ellis Island** ____/12

Your family is visiting New York. You would like to go to Ellis Island. You've read about it online and made notes. Use your notes to answer your family's questions.

You: Ich schlage vor, dass wir Ellis Island besuchen!

Brother: Was ist das?

You: ______________________________ (2 P)

Sister: Und was passierte denn dort?

You: ______________________________ (2 P)

Mother: Oh, das klingt interessant. Was kann man da machen?

You: ______________________________ (4 P)

Father: Das ist eine Insel? Wie kommt man da hin?

You: ______________________________ (1 P)

Mother: Was kostet es?

You: ______________________________ (1 P)

Father: Und das ist nur für die Fähre?

You: ______________________________ (2 P)

Mother: Ich bin dafür!

Ellis Island

- Point where 12 million immigrants entered U.S. by ship 1892–1924
- Papers and health checked there
- On the island:
  - Museum: photos / objects
  - Immigration centre with information about ships and their passengers
  - Interactive display of photos of museum visitors
  - Documentary film about families who came to U.S.
- Ferry from Battery Park
- Tickets online or at park
- Adults $18.50, kids under 12 $9.00
- Tickets = ferry + Ellis Island and Liberty Island (need extra ticket to go in statue)
- Airport-type checks

7 GUIDED WRITING A trip to Ellis Island

____/15

Write an e-mail to your American cousin about your family's trip to Ellis Island. Tell him/her

- what Ellis Island is.
- about something funny/strange that happened on the ferry.
- about the most interesting thing you saw there and why you liked it.

Write 120 words or more.

These phrases can help you:

That's where ...
On the ferry there was / we saw / suddenly / ...
The funniest thing happened ...
I really liked ...
You can ...
There was a really cool ...
The most interesting thing was ...
I liked it because ...

LERNTIPP

In dieser Aufgabe musst du sowohl Fakten wiedergeben (was Ellis Island ist, was man dort tun kann) als auch kreativ sein. Die Informationen in Aufgabe 7 helfen dir, etwas über die Fahrt und die Insel zu erzählen. Schmücke diese Fakten mit deinen eigenen Ideen aus, um alle Punkte der Aufgabe zu erfüllen.

Land of the free?
Schulaufgabe A

Unit **2**

Gesamtpunktzahl _____ / 67   Note _____

1 **READING** **Climate demonstration**   _____ / 10

Read this newspaper article. Then complete the task.

Climate[1] Demonstration in New York City

As part of an international movement of young people against climate change[2], more than 60,000 students took part in a protest in New York City on September 20, 2019. Millions more protested in 150 countries around the world.

The star of New York's event was 16-year-old Greta Thunberg, who had travelled from her native Sweden to the city to go to a climate meeting at the United Nations[3]. Thunberg began climate demonstrations in 2018. She sat outside the Swedish parliament during school hours. She said there was no reason to go to school if the planet is dying.

Greta has autism[4] and has been interested in the environment since the third grade. She calls her autism a superpower and says that it helps her to concentrate on this work.

After Greta began her strikes, first her classmates and later young people around the world joined her. Many take part in "Fridays for Future" demonstrations every week. Protesters are angry that world leaders are not doing enough to stop climate change.

Thunberg travelled to the U.S. in August on a boat and not on a plane because it's better for the environment. Three days before her speech at the United Nations she spoke to the crowd at the New York protest from

Battery Park. She said, "This is an emergency. Our house is on fire."

Starting in Foley Square, protesters held signs with messages such as "There is no Plan(et) B" or "I want a green future!" The demonstration continued through Lower Manhattan to Battery Park.

Other speakers included 20-year-old Xiuhtezcatl Martinez, an indigenous musician who has been fighting climate change for over ten years. "A [big] part of Thunberg's message is 'This is not for me,'" Martínez said.

New York City students could go to the protest and not to school if their parents said it was all right. Some people didn't agree with the decision to let students miss school, saying that the schools were supporting one side politically. However, over 87% of students did go to school that day.

[1]**climate** ['klʌɪmət] Klima [2]**climate change** Klimawandel [3]**United Nations** die Vereinten Nationen [4]**autism** ['ɔːtɪzəm] Autismus

Are the sentences below true (T) or false (F)? Choose 'Not in the text' (N) if there is not enough information to answer 'True' or 'False'. Tick (√) the correct answer.

	T	F	N
1 Half a million students took part in the "Friday for Future" demonstration in New York City on September 20, 2019.	☐	☐	☐
2 New York City students demonstrate every Friday.	☐	☐	☐
3 Greta Thunberg travelled to New York City for the march.	☐	☐	☐
4 Thunberg's autism has made it difficult for her to fight climate change.	☐	☐	☐
5 Since 2018, more and more students have joined Thunberg's protests.	☐	☐	☐
6 Greta sailed to the US.	☐	☐	☐
7 Thunberg spoke in Foley Square.	☐	☐	☐
8 Xiuhtezcatl Martinez is a good friend of Thunberg's.	☐	☐	☐
9 If their parents agreed, it was OK for students to miss school and go to the protest.	☐	☐	☐
10 Most students in New York City went to the march.	☐	☐	☐

USE OF ENGLISH

2 LANGUAGE Moviemaking ____/10

Ellison is giving Mabel advice about making a movie. Complete the sentences by filling in the correct form of each verb to make type 0, 1 or 2 *if*-sentences. You may need to add a modal verb.

1 If I ____________ *(be)* you, I would rewrite the script.

2 If you ____________ *(shoot)* in the morning, the light is better.

3 If the camerawork is good, they ____________ *(win)* a prize.

4 The soundtrack ____________ *(be)* awesome if she could use this song on it.

5 They ____________ *(see)* his eyes better if we shoot a close-up.

6 If you want to show the setting, ____________ *(use)* a long shot.

7 If I ____________ *(be)* you, I would use a medium shot at the beginning of the next scene.

8 ____________ *(stop)* shooting if the background noise is too loud.

9 Scenes ____________ *(be)* boring if they're too long.

10 If we ____________ *(have)* more money, we could pay our actors more.

3 WORDS Native Americans

___/11

Read the definitions below and find the words in the grid. Circle them and write each word on the line next to its definition. There are three words in the grid that you don't need.

1 connected with people who lived in a country before other people, especially white people, came there ______________________

2 from a particular place rather than coming to it from somewhere else ______________________

3 an area of land in the U.S. where only Native Americans live ______________________

4 a person of greater age and experience ______________________

5 having to do with or belonging to a group of Native Americans ______________________

6 Native Americans wear it on their heads on special days ______________________

7 objects like rings and earrings that people wear as decoration ______________________

8 a way to style long hair, using three parts ______________________

9 one of many soft light parts covering a bird's body ______________________

10 a small piece of glass, wood, etc. with a hole in it that you wear as part of jewellery ______________________

11 a leader of a group of people ______________________

N	I	S	W	A	M	P	X	T	Z	R
Q	O	N	A	T	I	V	E	F	L	E
S	P	I	D	A	E	B	O	R	J	L
S	S	F	T	I	G	H	W	E	N	I
E	A	E	M	A	G	I	W	D	P	G
R	C	A	K	T	V	E	T	L	V	I
D	R	T	A	F	L	R	N	E	B	O
D	E	H	D	L	I	U	E	O	H	N
A	D	E	E	B	Z	D	W	S	U	M
E	B	R	A	I	D	O	S	D	E	S
H	Y	L	V	C	H	I	E	F	T	R

4 WORDS Say it in English

____/5

Was sagst du auf Englisch, wenn du …

1 … sagen willst, dass deine Ur-Großmutter die Schule abgebrochen hat?

____

2 … deinen Bruder fragen willst, wann er gestern Nacht eingeschlafen ist?

____

3 … sagen möchtest, dass du die Prüfung bestehst, wenn du viel dafür lernst?

____

4 … sagen willst, dass du schon seit 5 Uhr wach bist?

____

5 … du erklären willst, dass die Anzahl der Schüler in deiner Schule um 10 % gestiegen ist.

____

LERNTIPP

Verwende das *present perfect (progressive)* oder *past perfect (progressive)*, um Sätze mit *since* zu bilden, z.B. *They've been married since December* oder *She had been working here since 1998.*

5 SKILLS Giving a presentation

____/7

Leonardo is giving a presentation about schools in the United States. Number the phrases of the presentation in the right order.

☐ My second slide shows some subjects that eighth graders typically take.

☐ Thank you all for your attention!

☐ This chart shows the structure of the schools.

☐ To start with, it's important to know a few basic facts about the structure of American schools.

☐ Today I'm going to talk about schools in the U.S.

☐ You can see here, for example, that all high schools go until the end of 12th grade.

☐ Good afternoon, everyone.

6 **MEDIATION** **A Native American exhibition** ___/9

Some Native American students are visiting your school. They have brought some things for an exhibition about their history and culture. Write the signs in German for them.

1 Before the Europeans arrived in North America, Native Americans made small bags from materials like leather and cloth to carry food, medicine, stones to start fires, etc. Native Americans quickly added European elements such as glass beads to their clothes and bags.

(4 P)

2 Moccasins are a kind of traditional Native American shoes and their name comes from native languages. There are many different types of moccasins: for example, in some areas it is important to wear shoes with hard bottoms. Each tribe has its own way of making and decorating moccasins.

„Moccasins" sind

(3 P)

3 For many Native American tribes it is important to use every part of an animal you shoot. They use feathers to decorate hair, clothes, hats and headdresses.

(2 P)

7 **GUIDED WRITING** **Saying goodbye** ____/ 15

Your mother got a great new job and your family is moving to a new town. You want to invite all of your friends to a big goodbye party. Write an email to send to them.

Tell them:

- about the move (reason, date, etc.)
- how you feel about moving
- when and where the party is
- what kind of party it is (pool party, quiet evening looking at photos, dance party, etc.)

Write about 120 words.

LERNTIPP

Es gibt im Englischen mehrere Möglichkeiten, um über die Zukunft zu reden. In vielen Situationen sind verschiedene Varianten möglich, wobei die Wahrscheinlichkeit und Einstellung des Redners bei jeder etwas anders gewichtet sind:
I'm going *to a new school in Texas.* (schon organisiert) / ***I'll go*** *to a new school in Texas.* (vermutlich) / ***I'm going to go*** *to a new school in Texas.* (ist fest geplant) / ***I'll be going*** *to a new school in Texas.* (werde ich in der Zukunft fortlaufend tun)

To: ______________________

Subject: ______________________

____

____

____

____

____

____

____

____

____

____

____

____

____

Land of the free?

Schulaufgabe B

Unit 2

Gesamtpunktzahl _____ / 84 Note _____

03

1 LISTENING A school debate

_____ / 14

The students at the Santa Ana Middle School are having a debate.
Listen and complete the tasks.

a Write the correct number in each box to match the speaker with his or her role in the debate. _____ / 7

1 Hayden Miller	A ☐	Is the first speaker for "Listen Up"
2 Avery Lind	B ☐	Is the last speaker in the debate
3 Juan Lozano	C ☐	Discusses the arguments made by "Listen Up"
4 Carley Presser	D ☐	Sums up for "Winning Arguments"
5 Hong Sun	E ☐	Presents the opening statements for "Winning Arguments"
6 Flynn Baker	F ☐	Disagrees with the statements made by "Winning Arguments"
7 Rachel Gofberg	G ☐	Chairperson

b What are the arguments of the two teams? Listen to the debate and complete the grid below. Be careful, one word is not enough. _____ / 7

	Winning Arguments	Listen Up
Argument 1	1 Gives everyone the chance to _____	4 Not everyone needs _____
Argument 2	2 Helps to _____	5 Cars are _____
Argument 3	3 Makes sure that teens learn to be _____	6 Time should be used _____
Argument 4		7 Cars will soon _____

USE OF ENGLISH

2 LANGUAGE Trail of Tears

____/ 6

Complete Sascha's summary of Trail of Tears with *reflexive pronouns* and *each other*. In some cases, either one can be used.

The story begins with the boy and his mother watching people rubbing ________________ on trees and putting mud on ________________ to say goodbye to their home. Some were crawling on their hands and knees on river stones. The boy knew they were sharp because he had hurt ________________ on them when he was younger.

Soldiers came and gave people blankets that were infected with a terrible disease. The boy's mother protected ________________ and her family and didn't let him take a blanket. Soldiers made the natives leave their homes and walk to Oklahoma. It was a long hard walk, but people helped ________________ . The boy's mother carried a baby who had died, because the baby's mother couldn't carry her any more. But then the boy's mother fell: she died that night. The family carried the mother's bones on the walk. The boy felt like the bones were carrying him and ________________ : his mother's spirit was lifting them.

3 LANGUAGE Preparing a presentation

____/ 6

Angelo is helping Natalia prepare her presentation. Rewrite each point as an *if*-sentence (type 0, 1 or 2). You may leave words out or add words to the new sentence.

1 Structure your presentation so people can understand it better.

If you structure ________________________________.

2 Sick people don't have to give their presentations.

If you were ________________________________.

3 Put your notes on cards so you can change the structure of your talk easily.

You can change ________________________________.

4 Mr Perez stops presentations that are longer than 10 minutes.

Mr Perez will stop ________________________________.

5 Mr Perez would give you an A for the best presentation.

If you gave ________________________________.

6 Don't give a boring presentation or people won't listen.

If you give ________________________________.

4 **WORDS** **A camping trip** ____/ 13

Eric is writing to his friend Jada about his family's camping trip. Complete the words in the texts.

How was your camping trip?

Not exactly a great e _ _ _ _ _ _ _ _ _ ! The whole area was like a s _ _ _ _: lots of m _ _ . We couldn't drive our car out of it and had to call a truck to p _ _ _ it out!

Oh no! Then what happened?

It was hard to make a c _ _ _ f _ _ _ because everything was wet. But we had a f _ _ _ _ _ _ _ c evening, talking and looking at the stars.

Sounds good!

But in the night, some noises woke us up. It was w _ _ _ _ _ howling[1] and they sounded very near! Isaac even thought he saw their s _ _ d _ _ _ outside.

What did you do?

Isaac was so scared that he wanted to sleep in the car. I was also a little worried about our s _ f _ _ _, so I went with him.

So you s _ _ v _ _ _ _ the night?

Of course. I'm writing to you! But in the morning our parents found f _ _ _ p _ _ _ _ _ on the ground: they thought they were from a p _ _ _ h _ _ ! That was the end of the camping trip. We all got back in the car and drove home!

A w _ _ _ decision!

[1](to) **howl** [haʊl] heulen, jaulen

5 WORDS Making things

___/15

How do you make these things? Write the words from the boxes in the correct spaces. You can use some words more than once. Make sure to use the correct form of each word. There are three words in the box that you don't need.

adobe · alcohol · bead · blanket · campfire · cloth · feather · fruit · hair · headdress · jewellery · leather · mud · silver · stone · vegetable · wood

1

You make ______________ with ______________.

2

These ______________ are made of ______________.

3

You need ______________ to build a ______________.

4
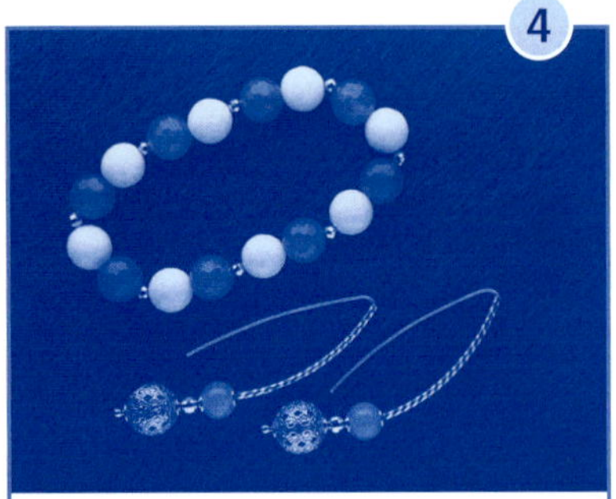

This ______________ is made of ____________ and ______________.

5

______________ is made of ______________, ______________, rice, etc.

6

A ______________ is made with ______________ and ______________.

6 GUIDED WRITING Asking for advice

___/15

You use a social media website on which members can post to groups to share experiences and ask for advice.

Your parents are unemployed and your family needs money. How can you help? Write a post to this group to ask for advice. Include the following:

- description of the problem (how it happened, when, why)
- an idea you have already tried
- ask for advice

Write about 120 words. Write the text in your exercise book.
Don't forget to write a suitable beginning and end.

7 **MEDIATION** **A Native American protest** ____/15

You have read an article about Native American protests. Your friend tried to read the article but didn't understand very much. Answer his questions.

The Dakota Access[1] Pipeline[2] protests

The Standing Rock reservation is one of the biggest in the United States. It goes through two states: North Dakota and South Dakota. Over 8,000 members of both the Lakota and Dakota tribes live there.

Every second family on the reservation lives in poverty. About 35% of the people are unemployed. There are many social and health problems, including suicide, especially of young people. There are also lots of problems with alcohol.

In 2016, North Dakota said a company could build a very long oil pipeline from North Dakota, through South Dakota and Iowa to Illinois. Part of the pipeline was under Lake Oahe and the Missouri River near the Standing Rock reservation.

In April of 2016, young people from Standing Rock and other Native American communities started protesting against the pipeline. The tribes on the reservation didn't want the pipeline under the lake and the river. Work on the pipeline might hurt places where their ancestors were buried and other sacred places. The indigenous people said they have to protect water: it's part of their religion.

Some young protestors started "prayer runs" all the way to Washington, D.C. to talk to politicians about the pipeline. They also used social media to get attention for their fight. About 25 adult protestors made a camp near the Missouri River. Thousands of people came to the camps to help protest.

In August 2016, protestors stopped the work on the pipeline. The next few months saw lots of problems between protestors, the oil company and police. The police stopped demonstrations. The oil company and police sometimes used violence against the protestors, for example they sprayed them with very cold water in the winter. The protests and the violence were frequently in the media.

The government stopped the construction in November 2016 to study the situation. But in January 2017 Donald Trump became president. He said the government should finish the study quickly. In February, the government said the oil company could finish the pipeline. The police made the protestors leave the camps that month.

Although the oil company built the pipeline, many young people think that their protests were important. They worked hard for their land and people and made the world notice their problems. In October 2019, Swedish teenage protestor Greta Thunberg visited Standing Rock. Tribal leaders gave her a prize for her work and an indigenous name that means "Woman who came from the skies[3]".

[1] **access** [ˈækses] Zugang [2] **pipeline** [ˈpaɪplaɪn] Leitung [3] **sky** [skaɪ] Himmel

1 Was ist Standing Rock und wo liegt es?

____

____ (2 P)

2 Wie ist die soziale Situation dort?

____

____ (2 P)

3 Wogegen wurde demonstriert?

____

____ (3 P)

4 In welchem Zeitraum fanden die Proteste statt?

____

____ (1 P)

5 Wer hat protestiert?

____

____ (2 P)

6 Wie haben sie demonstriert? (Nenne drei Aspekte.)

____

____

____

____

____ (3 P)

7 Wie ist es ausgegangen?

____

____ (2 P)

A changing world

Schulaufgabe A

Unit 3

Gesamtpunktzahl _____ / 66 Note ____

1 **READING** **Virtual … or reality?** _____ / 11

Read the story. Then complete the tasks.

Nina pulled her new virtual reality headset out of the box. She couldn't wait to try it! She quickly connected the headset to her TV system. Nina wasn't a big fan of games, but she had already downloaded a few "experiences" for her new headset.

The headset was all-in-one, with a built-in microphone and headphones. She put it on, happy that it was light and comfortable. **A** Nina looked at the screen and chose the national park experience: here in the city, she didn't see too much nature.

Suddenly, Nina was on a path. Amazing! **B** She looked around herself at the thousands of realistic details: the trees, the sound of birds and even the smell of earth and flowers. Wait … what? Smell? How could she smell something that wasn't real?

Nina took a couple of careful steps. She heard her feet and … felt stones and leaves under them. This was getting stranger and stranger! She pulled off her headset and looked around her living room. Still there.

Did she really want to go into the park again? Of course! She put the headset back on. Back in the park, she heard the sound of water and followed the path. **C** After a few minutes, she couldn't believe what she saw. A waterfall as high as a house dropped into a natural pool of clear blue water. Nina walked to the pool. The air was very warm, and Nina was starting to sweat … and the pool looked cool and inviting. She kicked off her shoes and moved towards the pool, putting a foot into the water. **D** It was wet!

Extremely surprised, Nina pulled the headset off. Back in her living room.
She thought for a moment. Should she go back? She absolutely wanted to. But was it safe? How could the water be wet? How could she smell the earth? She didn't understand.
Nina looked at the box the headset came in. "Realistic graphics!" it said. "Amazing sound!" **E**
She knew she had to go back. The experience was too wonderful to miss. She quickly set the headset back on her head.
Nina was back at the waterfall. **F** She made a cup out of her hands and filled them with water. She drank, feeling the cool water in her mouth. This was not virtual: this was reality!
Suddenly, she heard a sound behind her. A big brown bear and two baby bears were walking towards her. Nina froze. What do you do when you see a bear? Nina was a city girl: she had no idea.
G And then she remembered … this was not actually reality! She pulled off her headphones and found herself back in her living room. If the national park experience was so realistic, she definitely didn't want to try any of the shooting games!

a **Five sentences have been removed from the story. Choose the correct gap (A–G) in the text for each of the sentences below (1–5). Write the correct letter of the gap after each sentence. There are two gaps which you do not need to use.** ___/5

1 Nothing about smelling and feeling things. ☐

2 It didn't seem like a cartoon or even a movie: it just looked like she was in a forest. ☐

3 As the bears walked towards her, she started to get really scared. ☐

4 It even fit over her glasses. ☐

5 She slowly walked into the pool, feeling the water around her feet, legs and knees. ☐

b **Complete the sentences.** ___/6

1 Nina ______________ video games.

2 Nina lives in a ______________ .

3 Nina can ______________ birds in the national park experience.

4 The pool looks welcoming to Nina because she's ______________ .

5 Nina doesn't understand how she can ______________ and ______________ things in the park.

6 Three ______________ surprise Nina at the pool.

USE OF ENGLISH

2 LANGUAGE Park information ____/15

a Complete the description of Bryce Canyon National Park. Use the *passive* of the *simple present*. ____/7

LERNTIPP

Das Passiv wird mit einer Form von *be* + Partizip Perfekt *(past participle)* gebildet.
Simple present: *am/is/are + past participle:* He sees her. *(active)* → She is seen (by him). *(passive)*
Simple past: *was/were + past participle*: He saw her. *(active)* → She was seen (by him). *(passive)*

1 Bryce Canyon National Park in Utah ______________________ *(know)* for its red hoodoos, which are rocks with special forms.

2 Talks about the park ______________________ *(hold)* every day by rangers.

3 Places with great views ______________________ *(find)* on the main road.

4 The park ______________________ *(experience)* on horses by many visitors.

5 In the winter, rooms ______________________ *(offer)* at the Sunset Hotel.

6 Trails ______________________ *(divide)* into three categories.

7 The trails ______________________ *(keep)* clean by park workers.

b Give more information about the history of the park. Use the *passive* of the *simple past*. ____/8

J.W. Humphrey was a U.S. Forest Service worker who (1) ______________________ *(send)* to Utah in 1915. When he saw Bryce's Canyon (which (2) ______________________ *(name)* after a man who lived in the area), he sent photos to the Forest Service. Articles (3) ______________________ *(write)* about it for magazines and newspapers. In 1916, he (4) ______________________ *(give)* $50 to improve the road to the canyon. By 1919, the canyon (5) ______________________ *(visit)* by its first tourists. Two hotels (6) ______________________ *(build)* in the 1920s. The canyon (7) ______________________ *(make)* a national monument by President Warren G. Harding in 1923. The size of the park (8) ______________________ *(increase)* by President Herbert Hoover in 1931.

4 WORDS Virtual reality goggles ___/7

Complete the sentences with verbs from the box. There are four verbs you don't need. Use the *imperative form* of each verb.

cut · cut out · download · invent · ~~make~~ · paint · print · put together · recycle · repair · solve · test

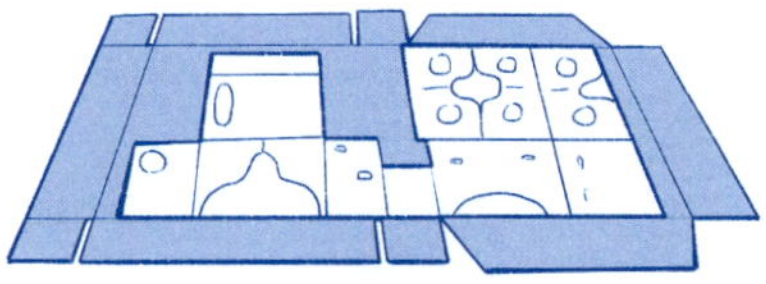

Make your own virtual reality goggles!

1 ______________ an old shoebox or other thin box and a plastic bottle.

2 ______________ a pattern from the internet on paper.

3 ______________ the box and bottle pieces, using the patterns.

4 ______________ the box pieces if you want.

5 ______________ the pieces ______________.

6 ______________ videos.

7 Put your phone in the goggles and ______________ them.

5 WORDS Radio programmes ___/8

Mack is listening to the radio. Match what he hears with the descriptions. There is one extra programme on the left.

1 ☐ Politicians will vote on a new gun control law today …

2 ☐ We'll see lots of snow today, with a high of around 25 degrees. Tomorrow we're looking at cooler weather …

3 ☐ A surprise announcement from Hollywood today! Dream team Brent Tipp and Christina Happy are getting married!

4 ☐ Two days after beating the Los Angeles Superstars, the Detroit Wolves easily won against the Oklahoma Panthers 89–47 last night …

5 ☐ Cigarettes? No, thank you! Did you know that smoking kills more …

6 ☐ Flat tyres? Our service team can be at your door in less than an hour. That's right: in about 60 minutes you'll be on the road again!

7 ☐ That was Anderton's newest hit, "Downtown Girls". Coming up, more of your favourites by Bobby Eyelash, Sweaty L. and No Way.

8 ☐ Bad news this morning, folks. Nothing is moving on most of the roads into the city due to several accidents caused by heavy snow …

A advert
B traffic news
C music programme
D weather report
E celebrity news
F sports news
G the news

GO»
AHEAD

REALSCHULE BAYERN

Schulaufgabentrainer
für Schülerinnen und Schüler

LÖSUNGEN

8

Deine Audios findest du auf www.scook.de.
Dort gibst du den unten stehenden Zugangscode in die Box ein.

Dein Zugangscode auf www.scook.de	**cb9ux-hwjq8**

Cornelsen

The American dream

Lösungen Schulaufgabe A

Unit 1

1 READING Noelle's New York City posts

1 *Because her family isn't going to spend a lot of time there.*
2 (two of these) *Clean; quiet; near Macy's and Times Square*
3 *Checked into the hotel and put their bags in their room*
4 *In movies*
5 *Noelle's favorite candy in a store in Times Square*
6 *To show souvenirs and ask friends how they like the Statues of Liberty*
7 *Theaters and musicals*
8 *A selfie of her with her favorite actor*

USE OF ENGLISH

2 LANGUAGE Writing the date

01

Hörtext:

1 March twenty-fifth, two thousand twenty-three
2 May nineteenth, two thousand nine
3 September twenty-third, sixteen thirty-two
4 February eighth, nineteen eighty-two
5 October fourteenth, twenty twenty-eight
6 June nineteenth, eighteen eighty-five

1 *March 25, 2023*
2 *May 19, 2009*
3 *September 23, 1632*
4 *February 8, 1982*
5 *October 14, 2028*
6 *June 19, 1885*

3 LANGUAGE The Statue of Liberty

a

1 ***Who*** gave the Statue of Liberty to the United States?
2 ***What*** do you have to do before you go into the statue?
3 ***Where*** does the statue stand?
4 ***Have*** you already booked tickets?
5 ***Did*** you go up to the statue's crown?
6 ***How*** many steps are in the statue?
7 ***Why*** did France give the statue to the U.S.?
8 ***Are*** you going to use the audio guide?
9 ***When*** was the statue opened to visitors for the first time?

b

1 As a symbol of friendship. ***7***
2 By boat. **–**
3 France. 1
4 Get your bags checked. ***2***
5 In 1886. ***9***
6 At night. **–**
7 Yes, I did. ***5***
8 354. ***6***
9 In New York Harbor. ***3***
10 No, I haven't. ***4***
11 Yes, I am. ***8***
12 No, she isn't. **–**

4 WORDS Volunteering at a shelter

I help out at a shelter for the ***homeless*** every Saturday in my ***neighborhood.*** Usually I help to give food to families. A lot of them lost their apartments because they got sick and didn't have ***insurance.*** They had to pay for doctors' bills and couldn't afford the ***rent.*** It isn't easy for kids living in a shelter: it's often ***noisy*** and there are a lot of ***strict*** rules. I'm always friendly and try to have fun with the little kids: working with them is a big ***responsibility.***

5 WORDS Around the city

1 *J*; 2 *F*; 3 *E*; 4 *B;* 5 *H*; 6 *A;* 7 *D*

6 SKILLS Filling in a form

ENTER INFORMATION Please give all answers in English.
Required fields are shown by an asterisk*.

APPLICANT / PASSPORT INFORMATION
Refer to your passport and enter all information in the same format.

Family Name*	First Name* *11*
Gender* ◉ Male ◉ Female	
Date of Birth* *1*	City of Birth* *4*
Country of Birth* *2*	Passport Number*
Country of Citizenship* *2*	National Identification Number
Issue Date* *5*	Issuing Country*
Personal Identification Number	Expiration Date* *9*

YOUR CONTACT INFORMATION
Please enter your contact information below.

Address Line 1* *6*	
Address Line 2	
Apartment Number	City* *4*
State/Province/Region*	Country* *2*
Telephone Type* *12*	Country Code + Phone*
Email Address*	

SOCIAL MEDIA (Optional)
Please enter information about your online activity.

Provider / Platform	*3*
Social Media Identity	

CONTACT INFORMATION WHILE IN THE U.S.

Name*	
Address Line 1*	
Address Line 2	
Apartment Number	
City*	*8*
State*	*8*
Phone* Number	

EMERGENCY CONTACT INFORMATION IN OR OUT OF THE U.S.
(family member or friend)

Family Name*	First (Given) Name* *7*
Email Address*	Telephone*

QUESTIONS
1 Do you have a physical or mental illness?*
Are you a drug user or addict?* *10*
Do you have a disease?*
2 Have you ever committed a crime that resulted in serious harm to property or another person?*

esta.cbp.dhs.gov

7 MEDIATION A taxi ride in New York City

Driver: How are you doing this morning?
You: ***Fine, thanks. And you?*** (1 P)
Driver: Not too bad, thanks! Where to?
You: Mama***, wo wollen wir hin?*** (1 P)
Mother: Oh, wie hieß es nochmal? Ich muss mal schauen … sorry, hätte ich vorher machen sollen. Moment mal …
You: ***Wait a minute, please. She's looking for the name of the hotel.*** (2 P)
Mother: Jetzt habe ich es … The Bryant Inn at Bryant Park.
You: ***We'd like to go to The Bryant Inn at Bryant Park.*** (1 P)
Driver: There's a lot of traffic this morning, so it'll take almost an hour.
You: ***Heute ist viel Verkehr auf den Straßen: Es wird fast eine Stunde dauern.*** (2 P)
Mother: Und wie viel kostet es?
You: ***How much will the fare be?*** (1 P)
Driver: Taxis from JFK airport to Manhattan always cost $52.
You: ***52 Dollar.*** (1 P)
Mother: Danke. Ich schließe mal so lange die Augen. Ich bin ganz müde!
Driver: Is your mother OK?
You: ***Yes, she's just tired!*** (1 P)
Driver: So, here we are: The Bryant Inn.
You: Mama, ***wir sind da.*** (1 P)
Mother: In Amerika gibt man mehr Trinkgeld als in Deutschland, also geben wir ihm 60 Dollar. Sag ihm, es stimmt so.

You: ***Here's 60 dollars. Keep the change.*** (2 P)
Driver: Thanks. Have a good day.
You: ***You too!*** (1 P)

8 **GUIDED WRITING** **A day in the Bronx**

Photo 1:
We took the subway to the Bronx to go to the zoo this morning. It took about 45 minutes. I loved the zoo, even though there were a lot of little kids there. The lion was my favorite animal there.

Photo 2:
We had a late lunch at a famous deli near the zoo. They had amazing sandwiches and great coffee (my dad said). They also had tasty cakes. Our waitress was really friendly, so my parents gave her a big tip!

Photo 3:
In the evening we went to a baseball stadium (also in the Bronx) to see a game. I'd never been to one before. The stadium was huge and there were masses of people. And the New York team won!

Zur Korrektur und Bewertung der ***Guided-Writing***-Aufgaben: Deine Lösung wird sicher anders lauten. Das macht nichts! Die Lösungsvorschläge sollen dir helfen, Ideen zum Thema zu finden. Lies sie dir mehrmals genau durch. Vielleicht kann dir jemand bei der Korrektur helfen. Manche Sätze kannst du vielleicht den Lösungsvorschlägen entsprechend korrigieren. Wenn du zu jedem Aspekt der Aufgabenstellung jeweils einen Satz fast fehlerfrei geschrieben hast, kannst du dir die volle Punktzahl anrechnen. Wenn es weniger Sätze sind, ziehst du dir für jeden fehlenden Satz einen Punkt ab, und wenn du mehr als einen Fehler in einem Satz gemacht hast, ziehst du dir auch jeweils einen Punkt ab. Deine Lehrkraft wird vielleicht anders werten. Die hier angegebene Wertung ist nur ein grobes Raster.

Unit 1

The American dream

Lösungen Schulaufgabe B

1 LISTENING Shopping trip

02

Hörtext:

Carlos: How are you doing this morning?
Shreya: Fine, thanks.
Carlos: My name is Carlos. Is there anything I can show you today?
Shreya: Well, I'd like some new makeup.
Carlos: You're definitely in the right place here in the cosmetics department! Have a seat: I can give you a demonstration of some of our new products.
Shreya: Oh, that would be great! I saw an ad for FeatureFace in a magazine and I love the colors!
Carlos: I do too! Working at FeatureFace was my dream job! Our products are the best!
Shreya: How long have you been working here?
Carlos: For about a year.
Shreya: How did you get the job? I would love to work here too!
Carlos: I filled in an application. Then the manager of the counter called me to come in for an interview with my résumé. And I got the job!
Shreya: That's so cool!
Carlos: Take a look in the mirror: how do you like the color I put on your cheeks?
Shreya: I love it! Can you do my eyes too? I saw a picture in the ad of a really pretty color: it was sort of blueish green. Do you know what I mean?
Carlos: Was it this color?
Shreya: I think that's it! What do you call it?
Carlos: They call this color Cyber Cyan. Unfortunately, I really don't think it would look good on you. Let's try this brown one instead.
Shreya: OK! I trust you!
Carlos: Just give me a minute ...
Shreya: These lightbulbs are so hot: I'm starting to sweat!
Carlos: I know, they really are hot. But they're good for putting on makeup. So ... almost finished ... there!
Shreya: Thank you! It looks excellent: you're a real pro!
Carlos: You're welcome!
Shreya: I'll take the eye makeup, please.
Carlos: Of course. That's $18.50.
Shreya: Let's see ... I only have a twenty.
Carlos: No problem: here's your change.
Shreya: I really appreciate your help!
Carlos: Oh, it was fun!
Shreya: Can you tell me where the restrooms are?
Carlos: Of course. Go past the entrance and up the escalator. They're on the second floor: just go straight ahead. If you can't find them, just ask one of the guards.

a

2 Carlos offers to demonstrate some products.

6 Shreya asks for directions to something in the store.

4 Shreya describes a color she would like to try.

1 Carlos introduces himself.

5 Shreya criticizes something.

3 Carlos describes how he got his job.

LERNTIPP

Aufgaben, bei denen du Sätze in die richtige Reihenfolge bringen musst, sind manchmal schwer zu bewerten. Wenn du eine Zahl falsch gesetzt hast, verschiebt sich die Nummerierung der kompletten Lösung – obwohl diese in Teilen trotzdem noch richtig sein kann. Achte bei der Überprüfung deiner Lösung auf diesen Aspekt.

b

1 Shreya is interested in FeatureFace makeup because she ***saw some colors she loved in a magazine.*** (1 P)
2 Carlos has been working at FeatureFace for ***about a year.*** (1 P)
3 To get the job, Carlos ***filled in an application*** (1 P) and ***brought his résumé to an interview.*** (1 P)
4 Cyber Cyan mixes ***blue*** and ***green.*** (1 P)
5 The light bulbs are so strong because it's better for ***putting on makeup.*** (1 P)
6 Shreya only buys ***eye makeup.*** (1 P)
7 Shreya asks for directions to ***the restrooms.*** (1 P)

USE OF ENGLISH

2 LANGUAGE Questions about a hotel

1 ***Who booked this hotel?***
2 ***Which elevator goes to our floor?***
3 ***Which rooms have the best view?***
4 ***What is on the key card?***
5 ***Who is paying the bill?***
6 ***What is making that noise?***

3 WORDS Deli customers

1 ***coffee addict***
2 Loves ***bagels***
3 In no ***state of mind*** to make a decision
4 Usually doesn't ***tip***
5 Really hates ***eggs***
6 Puts ***mustard*** on everything
7 Never has enough money for the ***bill***
8 ***Nickname:*** Big Mouth

4 WORDS Good news!

Today was a great day! My ***mom*** *(a short form of "mother")* found an ***apartment*** *(a set of rooms for living in)* we can afford in our old ***neighborhood/borough*** *(an area of a town or city)*! It's clean, no ***roaches*** *(a large brown insect that lives in buildings, especially if they are not clean)* … and best of all, it's not a ***shelter*** *(a building where people without a home can stay)*! We can take all of our ***property*** *(the things that you own)* over there next week and move in. It'll be great not to be ***homeless*** *(without a place to live)* any more. No ***curfew*** *(a time at which sb. must be home in the evening)*, no horrible living ***conditions*** *(the situation in which people live, work or do things)*, no sharing a ***bathroom*** *(a room in which there is a toilet and water to wash yourself)* with strangers! My sister and I will have to share a bedroom, but it has two ***closets*** *(a small room in a larger room; you can put clothes and other things in it)*. I'm really looking forward to leaving this place! I think everything is going to be ***all right*** *(OK)* now.

5 SKILLS Another way to say it

1 ***It's a yellow sauce you can put on a hot dog. It's spicy.***
2 ***You put it in a lamp, and it makes light.***
3 ***It's a little book with your photo in it. You use it when you go to another country.***
4 ***You put it in your hair to make a hairstyle.***
5 ***You use it to call people when you're not at home.***
6 ***You put it on your face to make yourself look prettier.***
7 ***It's a hot brown drink, but it's not tea.***
8 ***It's a place you can buy good food to eat there or bring home.***

6 MEDIATION Information about visiting Ellis Island

You: Ich schlage vor, dass wir Ellis Island besuchen!
Brother: Was ist das?
You: ***Das ist die Insel, auf der in den Jahren 1892 bis 1924 12 Millionen Einwanderer in den USA angekommen sind.*** (2 P)
Sister: Und was passierte denn dort?
You: ***Ihre Papiere wurden kontrolliert und es gab eine Gesundheits-untersuchung.*** (2 P)
Mother: Oh, das klingt interessant. Was kann man da machen?
You: ***Es gibt ein Museum mit Fotos und Objekten, ein Einwandererzentrum mit Informationen über die Schiffe und ihre Passagiere, ein inter-***

aktives Display / einen interaktiven Bildschirm mit Fotos von Besuchern und einen Dokumentarfilm über Familien, die in die USA eingewandert sind. (4 P)

Father: Das ist eine Insel? Wie kommt man da hin?

You: ***Mit einer Fähre von Battery Park.*** (1 P)

Mother: Was kostet es?

You: ***$18,50 für Erwachsene und $9,00 für Kinder, die jünger als 12 Jahre sind.*** (1 P)

Father: Und das ist nur für die Fähre?

You: ***Nein, auch für die Insel. Man kann mit der Karte auch Liberty Island besuchen, aber nicht in die Freiheitsstatue rein. Dafür braucht man eine zusätzliche Karte.*** (2 P)

Mother: Ich bin dafür!

7 GUIDED WRITING A trip to Ellis Island

Mögliche Lösung:

Hi there!
Today my family went to Ellis Island for the day. That's where a lot of immigrants first arrived in New York from 1892 until 1924. It's a museum now. On the ferry there was a passenger giving a manicure to his friend. My sister and I thought that was a really strange thing to do on a ferry! But his hands looked good!
I really liked the immigration center. You can find out about passengers who came to the U.S. I like to think about their lives and why they immigrated. I hope they all found a better life in America!
We have to go home in two days. I'll be sad to leave the city: it's so cool here!
Love,
Lena

Zur Korrektur und Bewertung der ***Guided-Writing***-Aufgaben s. S. 5 hier in den Lösungen.

Land of the free?

Lösungen Schulaufgabe A

Unit **2**

1 READING Climate demonstration

True: *5, 6, 9*
False: *1, 3, 4, 7, 10*
Not in the text: *2, 8*

USE OF ENGLISH

2 LANGUAGE Moviemaking

1 If I ***were*** you, I would rewrite the script.
2 If you ***shoot*** in the morning, the light is better.
3 If the camerawork is good, they ***might/could/will win*** a prize.
4 The soundtrack ***would be*** awesome if she could use this song on it.
5 They ***will/could see*** his eyes better if we shoot a close-up.
6 If you want to show the setting, ***use*** a long shot.
7 If I ***were*** you, I would use a medium shot at the beginning of the next scene.
8 ***Stop*** shooting if the background noise is too loud.
9 Scenes ***are*** boring if they're too long.
10 If we ***had*** more money, we could pay our actors more.

LERNTIPP

Wenn du Hilfe zu den ***if*-Sätzen** benötigst, findest du sie in deinem Schülerbuch im **Language File 6** auf S. 142–143.

3 WORDS Native Americans

1 *native*
2 *indigenous*
3 *reservation*
4 *elder*
5 *tribal*
6 *headdress*
7 *jewellery*
8 *braid*
9 *feather*
10 *bead*
11 *chief*

N	I	S	W	A	M	P	X	T	Z	R
Q	O	N	A	T	I	V	E	F	L	E
S	P	I	D	A	E	B	O	R	J	L
S	S	F	T	I	G	H	W	E	N	I
E	A	E	M	A	G	I	W	D	P	G
R	C	A	K	T	V	E	T	L	V	I
D	R	T	A	F	L	R	N	E	B	O
D	E	H	D	L	I	U	E	O	H	N
A	D	E	E	B	Z	D	W	S	U	M
E	B	R	A	I	D	O	S	D	E	S
H	Y	L	V	C	H	I	E	F	T	R

4 WORDS Say it in English

1 *My great-grandmother dropped out of school.*
2 *When did you fall asleep last night?*
3 *I'll pass the test if I study a lot (for it).*
4 *I've been awake since 5 o'clock.*
5 *The number of students at my school has increased by 10%.*

5 SKILLS Giving a presentation

6 | 7 | 4 | 3 | 2 | 5 | 1

LERNTIPP

Aufgaben, bei denen du Sätze in die richtige Reihenfolge bringen musst, sind manchmal schwer zu bewerten. Wenn du eine Zahl falsch gesetzt hast, verschiebt sich die Nummerierung der kompletten Lösung – obwohl diese in Teilen trotzdem noch richtig sein kann. Achte bei der Überprüfung deiner Lösung auf diesen Aspekt.

6 MEDIATION A Native American exhibition

1 *Als die ersten Europäer nach Nordamerika kamen, hatte die Kleidung der Ureinwohner noch keine Taschen. Stattdessen benutzten sie kleine Säcke/Beutel aus Materialien wie Leder und Stoff, um Sachen wie Lebensmittel, Medizin/Medikamente, Feuersteine usw. zu transportieren. Aber bald verwendeten sie europäische Dinge wie Glasperlen.* (4 P)

2 „Moccasins" sind *traditionelle Schuhe der amerikanischen Ureinwohner. Der Name kommt auch aus den Sprachen der Ureinwohner. Es gibt verschiedene Arten von „moccasins", z. B. mit harten Sohlen für bestimmte Böden. Jeder Stamm macht und verziert die Schuhe auf seine eigene Weise.* (3 P)

3 *Viele Ureinwohner legen großen Wert darauf, alle Teile von getöteten Tieren zu verwenden. Auch die Federn werden verwendet, z. B. um Kleidung oder Haare zu schmücken.* (2 P)

7 GUIDED WRITING Saying goodbye

Mögliche Lösung:

To:

Subject:

Hi everyone,

Big news today! My mother got a new job in Los Angeles … and my family is moving there next month! I know that it's very fast, but they want her to start right away. Our new house looks amazing (it even has a pool!), but I'm really going to/I will really miss you all! Although it's hard to move, I know it's the best thing for our family.

To say goodbye to all of you, I'm having a big party at my house on July 28th. You can come any time after 3 pm. We'll order pizza, watch our favorite movies, go to sleep at about three in the morning ;-) and have my dad's famous waffles for breakfast.

Let me know if you can come!

Love,

Mike

Zur Korrektur und Bewertung der ***Guided-Writing***-Aufgaben s. S. 5 hier in den Lösungen.

Land of the free?

Lösungen Schulaufgabe B

Unit 2

1 LISTENING A school debate

03

Hörtext:

Hayden Miller:

Good morning, everyone! Welcome to our debate on the topic "Schools should teach driving". I'm Hayden Miller, the chairman of the debate. Our two teams are "Winning Arguments" and "Listen Up". First, "Winning Arguments" will give arguments in favor of this idea.

Avery Lind:

Thank you, Chairman Miller. Good morning, everyone. I'm Avery Lind.
The job of schools is to prepare students for life as adults. Teaching driving does this in several ways.
Firstly, it's important that everyone has the chance to learn to drive. Lots of teens have families who can't afford to pay for driving lessons. If schools teach driving, then everyone has the chance to learn this important skill.
Secondly, many jobs require driving. It's easier and cheaper to get a driver's license than to go to college. Teaching driving in high school will help students get better jobs.
Thirdly, not every driving school is very good. Teaching driving in schools will help make sure that teens really learn how to be safe drivers.

Hayden Miller:

Thank you, "Winning Arguments".
"Listen Up" may now present arguments against the idea "Schools should teach driving".

Juan Lozano:

Chairman Miller, thank you very much.
I'm Juan Lozano for "Listen Up". We believe that schools should not be teaching driving.
Firstly, not everyone needs to know how to drive. Some people don't need a car because they live in a city and some people just don't want to drive or are even scared of driving.
Secondly, driving is bad for our environment! It uses gas and oil and makes the air dirty. It's much better to use bikes or public transport. Driving is also more dangerous than public transport.
Thirdly, teaching driving would use time that would be better spent on more important subjects like English, math and science.
Fourthly, soon we won't need to know how to drive! Cars will drive themselves. That will be much safer, and we can use our time in the car to read, watch a movie or even sleep.

Hayden Miller:

Thank you, "Listen Up". Now "Winning Arguments" has the chance to ask "Listen Up" questions and talk about their arguments.

Carley Presser:

Thank you, Chairman Miller.
My name is Carley Presser. It's true that not everyone needs to drive. But high schools offer many courses that not every student has to take. Driving courses don't need to be required, but they should be offered.
It's not possible for everyone to use public transport or bikes. People who live on farms, for example, can't do that.
We think that cars that drive themselves sound great, but we don't know if and when everyone will have one. For now, we need to drive ourselves.

Hayden Miller:

Thank you, "Winning Arguments".
"Listen Up", it's your turn.

Hong Sun:
Hi, I'm Hong Sun.
We don't agree that the schools should pay for students to learn to drive. It costs a lot of money to develop courses, hire teachers and pay for materials. We think that people who want to learn how to drive should pay for it themselves.
We also think that better laws about private driving schools would make sure that the schools do a good job. We don't need to give high schools that job.

Hayden Miller:
"Winning Arguments", you may now sum up.

Flynn Baker:
My name is Flynn Baker.
Of course, it takes a lot of money to pay for driving classes in schools. But the cost of accidents and unemployment are much higher! We believe that making good driving lessons available to everyone is part of building a strong and safe country.

Hayden Miller:
"Listen Up", you may finish now.

Rachel Gofberg:
I'm Rachel Gofberg.
Our position is that driving lessons are not important enough to teach in school. Reading, math, science … those are the important subjects our schools should teach. If you want to learn to drive, you should do it in your own time, with your own money.

a

A *3* Is the first speaker for "Listen Up"

B *7* Is the last speaker in the debate

C *4* Discusses the arguments made by "Listen Up"

D *6* Sums up for "Winning Arguments"

E *2* Presents the opening statements for "Winning Arguments"

F *5* Disagrees with the statements made by "Winning Arguments"

G *1* Chairperson

b

	Winning Arguments	Listen Up
Argument 1	1 Gives everyone the chance to ***learn how to drive.***	4 Not everyone needs ***to learn how to drive.***
Argument 2	2 Helps to ***get better jobs.***	5 Cars are ***bad for the environ-ment.***
Argument 3	3 Makes sure that teens learn to be ***safe drivers.***	6 Time should be used ***for more important subjects.***
Argument 4		7 Cars will soon ***drive themselves.***

USE OF ENGLISH

2 LANGUAGE Trail of Tears

The story begins with the boy and his mother watching people rubbing ***themselves*** on trees and putting mud on ***each other/themselves*** to say goodbye to their home. Some were crawling on their hands and knees on river stones. The boy knew they were sharp because he had hurt ***himself*** on them when he was younger.
Soldiers came and gave people blankets that were infected with a terrible disease. The boy's mother protected ***herself*** and her family and didn't let him take a blanket.
Soldiers made the natives leave their homes and walk to Oklahoma. It was a long hard walk, but people helped ***each other***. The boy's mother carried a baby who had died, because the baby's mother couldn't carry her any more.

But then the boy's mother fell: she died that night. The family carried the mother's bones on the walk. The boy felt like the bones were carrying him and ***themselves***: his mother's spirit was lifting them.

3 LANGUAGE Preparing a presentation

1 If you structure ***your presentation, people can understand it better.***
2 If you were ***sick, you wouldn't have to give your presentation.***
3 You can change ***the structure of your talk easily if you put your notes on cards.***
4 Mr Perez will stop ***your presentation if it's longer than 10 minutes.***
5 If you gave ***the best presentation, Mr Perez would give you an A.***
6 If you give ***a boring presentation, people won't listen.***

LERNTIPP

Wenn du Hilfe zu den ***if*-Sätzen,** benötigst, findest du sie in deinem Schülerbuch im **Language File 6** auf S. 142–143.

4 WORDS A camping trip

How was your camping trip?

Not exactly a great ***experience***! The whole area was like a ***swamp***: lots of ***mud***. We couldn't drive our car out of it and had to call a truck to ***pull*** it out!

Oh no! Then what happened?

It was hard to make a ***campfire*** because everything was wet. But we had a ***fantastic*** evening, talking and looking at the stars.

Sounds good!

But in the night, some noises woke us up. It was ***wolves*** howling and they sounded very near! Isaac even thought he saw their ***shadows*** outside.

What did you do?

Isaac was so scared that he wanted to sleep in the car. I was also a little worried about our ***safety***, so I went with him.

So you ***survived*** the night?

Of course. I'm writing to you! But in the morning our parents found ***footprints*** on the ground: they thought they were from a ***panther***! That was the end of the camping trip. We all got back in the car and drove home!

A ***wise*** decision!

5 WORDS Making things

1 You make ***adobe*** with ***mud***.
2 These ***blankets*** are made of ***cloth***.
3 You need ***wood*** to build a ***campfire***.
4 This ***jewellery*** is made of ***beads*** and ***silver***.
5 ***Alcohol*** is made of ***fruit***, ***vegetables***, rice, etc.
6 A ***headdress*** is made with ***feathers*** and ***beads***.

6 GUIDED WRITING Asking for advice

Hi guys. I have a problem and I'd like some advice from you. My parents are unemployed and my family needs money. My mother lost her job last year when her company closed. My father can't work because he has been sick for a few years. We have a flat and food, but no money for things like cool clothes or holidays. I sometimes do jobs for our neighbours, like washing their cars or mowing their grass, but I don't get very much money for that. How can I earn some money to buy nice things and help my parents? I know that you

always have a lot of good ideas. I'm looking forward to hearing them!
Yours, Alex

> Zur Korrektur und Bewertung der ***Guided-Writing***-Aufgaben s. S. 5 hier in den Lösungen.

7 MEDIATION A Native American protest

1 *Standing Rock ist ein Reservat für amerikanische Ureinwohner. Es erstreckt sich über North und South Dakota.* (2 P)
2 *Es gibt ungefähr 8.000 Einwohner. Viele sind sehr arm und arbeitslos. Es gibt viele soziale Probleme, z. B. Selbstmord und Alkoholmissbrauch.* (2 P)
3 *Gegen den Bau einer Ölleitung in der Nähe von Gewässern, Grabstätten und anderen heiligen Orten der Ureinwohner.* (3 P)
4 *Sie haben im Frühjahr 2016 begonnen und gingen bis Februar 2017.* (1 P)
5 *Am Anfang waren es junge Ureinwohner, aber Tausende erwachsene Demonstranten kamen im Laufe der nächsten Monate dazu.* (2 P)
6 *Die Jugendlichen haben „Gebetsläufe" gemacht und sind bis nach Washington D.C. gelaufen, um mit Politikern zu sprechen. Sie haben auch soziale Medien genutzt, um Aufmerksamkeit zu bekommen. Die erwachsenen Demonstranten haben Lager errichtet und haben auch die Bauarbeiten verhindert.* (3 P)
7 *Die Demonstranten haben verloren: Unter Präsident Donald Trump wurde die Leitung gebaut.* (2 P)

A changing world

Lösungen Schulaufgabe A

Unit **3**

1 READING Virtual … or reality?

a

1 *E*; 2 *B*; 3 *G*; 4 *A*; 5 *F*

b

1 Nina ***doesn't like*** video games.
2 Nina lives in a ***city***.
3 Nina can ***hear*** birds in the national park experience.
4 The pool looks welcoming to Nina because she's ***warm/hot***.
5 Nina doesn't understand how she can ***feel*** and ***smell*** things in the park.
6 Three ***bears*** surprise Nina at the pool.

USE OF ENGLISH

2 LANGUAGE Park information

a

1 Bryce Canyon National Park in Utah ***is known*** for its red hoodoos, which are rocks with special forms.
2 Talks about the park ***are held*** every day by rangers.
3 Places with great views ***are found*** on the main road.
4 The park ***is experienced*** on horses by many visitors.
5 In the winter, rooms ***are offered*** at the Sunset Hotel.
6 Trails ***are divided*** into three categories.
7 The trails ***are kept*** clean by park workers.

b

J.W. Humphrey was a U.S. Forest Service worker who (1) ***was sent*** to Utah in 1915. When he saw Bryce's Canyon (which (2) ***was named*** after a man who lived in the area), he sent photos to the Forest Service. Articles (3) ***were written*** about it for magazines and newspapers. In 1916, he (4) ***was given*** $50 to improve the road to the canyon. By 1919, the canyon (5) ***was visited*** by its first tourists. Two hotels (6) ***were built*** in the 1920s. The canyon (7) ***was made*** a national monument by President Warren G. Harding in 1923. The size of the park (8) ***was increased*** by President Herbert Hoover in 1931.

4 WORDS Virtual reality goggles

1 ***Recycle*** an old shoebox or other thin box and a plastic bottle.
2 ***Print*** a pattern from the internet.
3 ***Cut out*** the box and bottle pieces, using the patterns.
4 ***Paint*** the box pieces if you want.
5 ***Put*** the pieces ***together.***
6 ***Download*** videos.
7 Put your phone in the goggles and ***test*** them.

5 WORDS Radio programmes

1 *G*; 2 *D*; 3 *E*; 4 *F*; 5 -; 6 *A*; 7 *C*; 8 *B*

6 MEDIATION Product review

Sister: Denkst du, diese Rezension ist gut?
You: ***Ja***, 237 Leute ***fanden sie hilfreich***. (1 P)
Sister: Kann man mit der Uhr telefonieren?
You: Ja, aber ***du brauchst eine SIM-Karte dafür***. (1 P)
Sister: Können unsere Eltern immer sehen, wo ich bin?
You: ***Ja, das können sie***. (1 P)
Sister: Gibt es die Uhr nur in Rot, wie auf dem Foto?
You: ***Nein, es gibt noch andere Farben***. (1 P)
Sister: Warum ist sie so teuer? Andere sind billiger.
You: ***Die Qualität soll besser als bei den anderen sein***. (1 P)
Sister: Muss man das Ding dauernd aufladen?
You: ***Nein. Sie meinen, der Akku bleibt lange geladen***. (1 P)
Sister: Wie ist die Kamera? Kann man Fotos auf der Uhr direkt bearbeiten?
You: ***Die Kamera ist offenbar nicht so gut. Aber es gibt viele Sticker, mit denen du deine Fotos gestalten kannst***. (3 P)
Sister: Dauert es lange, die Uhr in Betrieb zu nehmen?
You: ***Hier steht, dass es ganz schnell geht***. (1 P)

7 GUIDED WRITING Car radio advert

Introducing the new 2022 Carter Star. The Star is beautiful inside and out. Offered in any colour you want, the sporty Star is great for showing your style. Because it's electric, the Star doesn't cause air pollution. The battery will take you over 100 miles when charged. Inside the car, there's enough room to carry you, your friends and your bags for a weekend trip.
The Star is full of intelligent technology: it remembers your favourite seat position and you can control the speakers, lights and more with your voice. You can connect your smartphone to the built-in stereo system and enjoy your favourite music on the Star's amazing speakers.
Order yours online today for just $25,999. Your new car will be brought to your front door in January.

Zur Korrektur und Bewertung der ***Guided-Writing***-Aufgaben s. S. 5 hier in den Lösungen.

A changing world

Unit 3

Lösungen Schulaufgabe B

1 LISTENING On the radio

04

Hörtext:

1

Woman: Teen star Minnie Billy Black has been volunteering at a homeless shelter in Los Angeles. Unnamed sources say she's preparing for a role as a homeless girl for her next movie.

Man: This isn't the first time Black has volunteered. She has been working with animal groups for years and she helped clean up one of the city's parks last month.

Woman: Black says that she is lucky to have such a good life and wants to help other people.

2

Man: Star basketball player LeRoy Jones has announced that he's moving from the Los Angeles Superstars to the Detroit Wolves.

Woman: So what's behind the move? I've heard Detroit offered him more money than he's getting in Los Angeles.

Man: Some people have also been saying that he's not happy with the team's coach. But Jones says that his girlfriend, a Detroit native, misses the city and asked Jones to change teams to be near her family.

3

Woman: We're giving away lots of prizes this week to celebrate our station's 25th birthday. The next three callers are all winners! Hello, caller number one, you're on the air!

Teenage boy:
Wow! I'm on the radio? What did I win? A CD?

Woman: Even better! We have a new internet radio for you so you can listen to our station everywhere! …
Let's go to our next caller. You've won two free tickets to Arinar's concert next week!

Teenage girl:
Thankyouthankyouthankyou! I love Arinar! I have posters of him all over my room.

Woman: I hope you have a great time! Next caller, we have Arinar tickets for you too … in the VIP section. And our celebrity car will take you to the show and back home!

4

Man: The Motor City has a new place to play. Come to Your Virtual Life, Detroit's first virtual reality center. Take a trip to the stars, dive to the bottom of the ocean or get together with friends to fight monsters and aliens. The possibilities are endless at Your Virtual Life.
Book your space online or walk in: Twelve rooms are waiting! Planning a party? A virtual reality experience is great for birthdays and other celebrations.
For more information, visit us online or call us at 313-555-9794.

5

Woman: Live from Detroit, I'm Cora Coles. After several accidents this year, Carter Cars will not sell its new Star model anymore. Experts first believed that the cars' tyres were causing the problems, but now think they're from the steering wheels. Robots on the company's assembly line may not have welded parts together correcly.

Male factory worker:
These robots can't do everything that people do! They're replacing a lot of workers, but I think that's a bad idea. They don't care about the products and they don't see everything that a person can see.

Woman: These aren't the first problems with the Star: drivers have also reported trouble with the engine.

6

Man: Good morning, guys! Hope you've got a lot of time this morning, because you're going to need it on the roads today! Heavy rain is making driving hard for everyone, but a six-car accident is causing even more trouble: police have closed the Ambassador Bridge because of it. No word yet on when it will be opened again. Work on the bridge has also meant slow traffic, but work is planned to be completed this Friday.

7

Woman: Let's take a look at the weather around Detroit this afternoon. Our station at Belle Isle is showing temperatures of around 80 degrees, so go there to enjoy a perfect afternoon at our city's best beach. Outside the city it's a little bit cooler, with lots of people relaxing in their yards. This weekend will bring lots of rain, so you might want to go to a movie theater instead of the beach. The sun will come back at the beginning of the week: just in time to miss it while you're in school or at work. Sorry!

1 *C*; 2 *B*; 3 *C*; 4 *B*; 5 *A*; 6 *A*; 7 *B*

USE OF ENGLISH

2 LANGUAGE Product review: Smart pillow

This pillow (1) ***was given*** to me as a birthday present last week. A lot of features (2) ***are included*** and some of them are very useful. Your sleep (3) ***is tracked*** by sensors in the pillow: you (4) ***are told*** every morning how long you have slept. However, my head (5) ***isn't/is not always recognized*** by the pillow, so this feature doesn't work every night.
On the first night I used it, I (6) ***was woken up*** by music in the middle of the night: the pillow (7) ***was switched on*** by the app accidentally!
(8) ***I'm/am reminded*** every night by the pillow to switch off the light, which is very helpful: I sometimes read in bed for hours and forget to sleep. And (9) ***I'm/am prevented*** from sleeping too long by the pillow's alarm!

3 LANGUAGE Visiting national parks

1 Climate change is warming up the planet, ***threatening*** our national parks.
2 ***Playing*** dead, a hiker survived an attack by a bear last year.
3 When ***volunteering***, Max tells visitors about the wolves in the park.
4 While ***climbing*** to the top of the mountain, I stopped to look at the view.
5 ***Growing*** to over 107 meters high, redwood trees are found in California and Oregon.
6 ***Tracking*** animals, scientists find out about more about the effects of climate change on their environment.
7 ***Taking part*** in extreme sports, some visitors have accidents in national parks.

4 WORDS Say it in English

1 ***My aunt works on the assembly line in the car factory.***
2 ***My seat is too far from the steering wheel.***
3 ***Do you want to listen to music with headphones or speakers?***
4 ***A new invention could reduce car accidents by 10%.***
5 ***Can you unlock your house with your smartphone?***

5 WORDS Two meanings

1 Shelby bought some purple **paint** to **paint** her car purple.
2 That broken **lock** won't **lock** your bike.
3 Our car **features** some of the newest smart **features**.
4 They **track** deer with this device while walking on the **track**.
5 Sometimes we know what **causes** accidents and sometimes we can't find any **causes**.
6 The police said his **speed** was over 100 miles an hour, but he usually doesn't **speed**.

7 She likes to talk with the other **volunteers** when she **volunteers** at the park.
8 I can **repair** it, but the **repair** probably won't last long.

6 SKILLS A review of Henry Ford Museum of American Innovation

Is the review easy to understand? ☻	*Good structure*
Is there enough information? ☻	*Information about what you can see, movie, food, etc.*
Is the opinion of the writer clear? ☻	*great, amazing, favorite, etc.*
Does the writer use different adjectives? ☻	*big, old, funny*
Are the ideas joined with linking words? ☹	*Don't start so many sentences with "There is/are/were": use words like "and" or "in addition" or "so" to link them.*
Is the grammar correct? ☹	*wrong verb form: "include" instead of "includes"*
Are the spelling and punctuation correct? ☹	*"plains" instead of "planes"* *"brake" instead of "break"*

7 MEDIATION Visiting a national park

Vater: Also, was sind diese *pictured rocks*? Und wo finden wir sie?
Du: ***Das sind große Steine am Strand mit sehr schönen gestreiften Farben und tollen Formen.*** (2 P)
Vater: Da müssen wir unbedingt hin! Was gibt es sonst hier für Landschaften?
Du: (give three examples) ***Wasserfälle, Wälder und Sümpfe*** (1 P)
Vater: Kann man hier mit Kindern gut wandern?
Du: ***Ja, besonders auf dem Munising Falls Weg. Oder man kann zum Mosquito Beach wandern.*** (2 P)
Vater: Prima. Was kann man noch alles im Park unternehmen?
Du: (give three examples) ***Man kann auch mit den Rangern eine Wanderung machen. Wir können angeln, ein Boot mieten, Vögel beobachten, uns am Strand entspannen oder nachts Sterne beobachten.*** (3 P)
Vater: Und was für Tiere gibt es hier?
Du: ***Man sieht vor allem Vögel und kleinere Tiere. Aber es gibt auch Rehe, Bären und Wölfe.*** (2 P)
Vater: Hier gibt's offenbar viel zu sehen und zu tun! Kann man hier auch zelten?
Du: ***Ja, aber dafür braucht man eine Reservierung.*** (1 P)
Vater: Das wusste ich nicht. Schade!

8 GUIDED WRITING Product review

Awesome product for flying fun
I bought the drone to take cool pictures of me and my friends from the air. I chose this one because it had a lot of good reviews and it wasn't too expensive.
This is my first drone, but I could start using it a few minutes after opening the box. The app is easy to install and use. The quality of the drone is great. I've crashed it about a million times already and it hasn't broken. Connecting with the drone works really well. It sends videos and photos to my smartphone while it's in the air and they look great.
One disadvantage of this drone is that it only stays in the air for about eight minutes: the battery doesn't last very long when you charge it. Another problem is that the drone always flies around, but sometimes I want it to take a few pictures or a video from one place. Also, if it flies too high, the connection with the phone is lost.
Overall, this drone is great for the price and a lot of fun.

Zur Korrektur und Bewertung der ***Guided-Writing***-Aufgaben s. S. 5 hier in den Lösungen.

Unit 4

Black lives

Lösungen Schulaufgabe A

1 READING Beyoncé Knowles

a

A *2*; B *3*; C *7*; D *1*; E *0*; F *4*

b

True: ***1, 6, 8, 10***
False: ***4, 5, 9***
Not in the text: ***2, 3, 7***

USE OF ENGLISH

2 LANGUAGE *Black Lives Matter*

1 We can explain the reasons for the movement to the class.
2 Let's show some pictures of protest marches to them.
3 Our teacher suggested this book to me.
4 Should we tell everyone the story of Trayvon Martin?
5 We can ask the class for their opinion about the movement.
6 I'll send you my slides tomorrow.
7 Please look for photos this weekend and give them to me on Monday.
8 Our town's newspaper didn't report this story to its readers.
9 Can you introduce the topic to the class?

3 LANGUAGE After Hurricane Katrina

Dear Luisa,
I ***was*** finally ***allowed*** time to use the computer here! We're in a shelter in Texas: we ***were given*** space here after we had left New Orleans. We've been here for a week now. My mother ***was sent*** money by friends and relatives, so I ***was bought*** some new clothes yesterday. We're leaving here tomorrow: my parents ***were offered*** an apartment near New Orleans by a friend.
I'm happy you're also OK. I ***was shown*** the e-mail your mother wrote to my mother. I ***was asked*** by my mother to say she'll answer soon.
Stay safe!
Tom

4 WORDS Blacks in the U.S.

Blacks in the U.S. have fought against (1) ***A*** for hundreds of years. The (2) ***C*** freed African-Americans from (3) ***D*** but (4) ***C*** in the south stopped them from getting the same (5) ***B*** and using the same facilities as whites. Even worse: unfair laws were (6) ***A*** which (7) ***B*** African-Americans from voting. The Civil Rights Act of 1964 made discrimination illegal. But even today African-Americans are (8) ***C*** of (9) ***D***: they are stopped more often than whites by the police because of their (10) ***A***.

5 WORDS Word families: Sport

1 ***Gymnasts*** are people who do gymnastics.
2 Talented people work hard to develop their ***talent(s)***.
3 The players were ***awarded*** awards.
4 The medalists wore their ***medals*** proudly.
5 I was in a lot of ***pain*** from my painful injuries.
6 The boxers were ***boxing*** in the ring.
7 The coaches ***coach*** the athletes every day.
8 Who was the champion of the last ***championship***?

6 GUIDED WRITING What's important to me

Mögliche Lösung:

One of the most special things I own is a ring that my grandmother gave to me. It's a small gold band with a pretty blue stone in it. It's very old: her parents gave it to her when she was my age.
This piece of jewellery is important to me because I know how much my grandmother loved it. Her family didn't have a lot of money, but they bought it for her 16th birthday. I'm very proud that my grandmother gave it to me. It shows me that she trusts me and that she thinks that I'm special and responsible.
I wear this ring every day: I never take it off. That way, I know that I'll never lose it. Seeing this circle of gold on my finger

reminds me of Grandmother and how much she loves me. And the ring is pretty! I get a lot of comments and questions about it. Some people want to know where I bought it. I'm happy that no one else has one like it.

Zur Korrektur und Bewertung der ***Guided-Writing***-Aufgaben s. S. 5 hier in den Lösungen.

7 MEDIATION Calling the doctor's office

Receptionist: Dr. Weingast's office. How can I help you?

You: ***I'd like to make an appointment, please.*** (1 P)

Receptionist: Is the appointment for you or for someone else?

You: ***It's for my brother.*** (1 P)

Receptionist: Can you please give me his name and date of birth?

You: *Name und Geburtsdatum des (fiktiven) kleinen Bruders nennen.* (1 P)

Receptionist: And what's the reason for the appointment?

You: *(Frag deinen Vater, was deinem Bruder fehlt.)* ***Papa, was hat er eigentlich?*** (1 P)

Father: Sein Bauch tut weh und er hat Fieber.

You: ***His stomach hurts and he has a high temperature.*** (1 P)

Receptionist: I have an appointment free in 45 minutes. Can you get here that quickly?

You: ***Sie hat in 45 Minuten einen freien Termin. Schaffen wir das?*** (2 P)

Mother: Das wird knapp. Ist das der einzige freie Termin?

You: ***Is that the only appointment you have?*** (1 P)

Receptionist: Yes, I'm sorry.

You: Ja.

Father: Sag ihr, wir sind in einer Dreiviertelstunde da.

You: ***We'll be there in 45 minutes.*** (1 P)

Receptionist: Does your brother have health insurance?

You: ***Hat er eine Krankenversicherung?*** (1 P)

Mother: Ja, hat er.

You: ***Yes, he does.*** (1 P)

Receptionist: Great. Please bring the documents with you. Goodbye.

You: Thank you. Goodbye.

Unit 4 Black lives

Lösungen Schulaufgabe B

1 LISTENING Stopped by the police

05

Hörtext:

Girl 1: Hey, do you hear that siren?
Girl 2: What? Oh, man … there's a police car behind us with its lights on!
Girl 3: Pull over, Clarissa!
Girl 2: What should I do?
Girl 1: Just keep your hands on the wheel. And Oona, put your hands on the dashboard.
Police officer: Good evening, girls.
Girls: Hi / Good evening / Hello.
Police officer: Can I see your license and registration, please?
Girl 2: Here's the registration. Can I get my license out of my wallet?
Police officer: Of course.
Girl 2: Here you go.
Police officer: What are you girls doing tonight?
Girl 2: We were studying at the library and now we're going to get some pizza.
Police officer: Sounds like a fun night! Did you have anyone else in the car with you tonight?
Girl 2: Anyone else? No. Oh, wait: My father rode with us to the library, but he didn't stay very long. He walked home.
Police officer: What time did you go to the library?
Girl 2: Um … My father and I left our house at 3 o'clock. Then I had to get Frances and Oona. So we got to the library at about 3:15. Is there a problem? Did I do something wrong?
Police officer: No. We got a call from a neighborhood watchman: He saw a car driving very slowly down his street and got suspicious.
Girl 2: That wasn't me. We just left the library a minute ago: we didn't drive down a street with houses.
Police officer: It was the same kind of car as yours. But he said there were boys in the car and there are only girls in your car. Don't worry: I'm not going to arrest you!
Girl 1: Is there a law against driving slowly down a street?
Police officer: No. But sometimes burglars drive slowly when they're looking for a house to steal from. Burglars have stolen things from that street a few times this month and the victims are being very careful.
Girl 3: I can understand that!
Police officer: Here are your documents. Have a good night, girls. Enjoy your pizza!
Girls: Thanks! / We hope you catch the burglars! / Good night!
Girl 2: I thought we were all going to prison tonight!
Girl 1: I thought you were driving too fast or didn't have your lights on!
Girl 3: It's good that you were so polite, Clarissa. She just wanted to make sure we aren't burglars.
Girl 2: And it's good that Frances reminded me to keep my hands on the wheel.
Girl 1: That's what the police officer who came to school last year told us, remember?
Girl 2: Yes! But I was so nervous that I forgot!

1 *C*; 2 *B*; 3 *C*; 4 *A*; 5 *D*; 6 *C*

USE OF ENGLISH

2 LANGUAGE What would have happened?

1 If Clarissa hadn't been playing music so loudly, ***she might/would/could have heard the police car earlier***.

2 The girls would have left the library earlier ***if they had got(ten) hungry***.
3 ***The police officer wouldn't have stopped Clarissa's car*** if it hadn't been the same kind as the other car.
4 Clarissa and her father could have gotten to the library earlier ***if they hadn't gone to her friends' houses***.
5 ***The watchman wouldn't/might not have been suspicious*** if there hadn't been burglars in the neighborhood recently.
6 ***The police officer would have arrested the girls*** if they had been the burglars.
7 The girls wouldn't have known how to behave ***if a police officer hadn't visited their school***.
8 Clarissa would have remembered to put her hands on the wheel ***if she hadn't been so nervous***.
9 ***Would you have been nervous*** if you had been driving the car?

3 LANGUAGE Marques had a hard day

1 School was really challeng***ing*** but not especially inspir***ing***.
2 After school, he had baseball practice, which was extremely tir***ing***.
3 His baseball coach is pretty relax***ed***, but his teammates aren't.
4 Marques is worri***ed*** about a test tomorrow. His last grade was disappoint***ing***.
5 He's also embarass***ed*** about something stupid he said in class.
6 It's not supris***ing*** that he's going to bed early. He'll feel energiz***ed*** in the morning.

4 WORDS Slavery in the United States

1 ***Africa***
2 ***They worked in fields / Field work***
3 ***The south***
4 ***Escape (slavery/to the north)***
5 ***The Civil War***
6 ***The north and the south***
7 ***The north***
8 ***He banned it. / He freed the slaves.***

5 WORDS Storms

Complete the crossword puzzle.

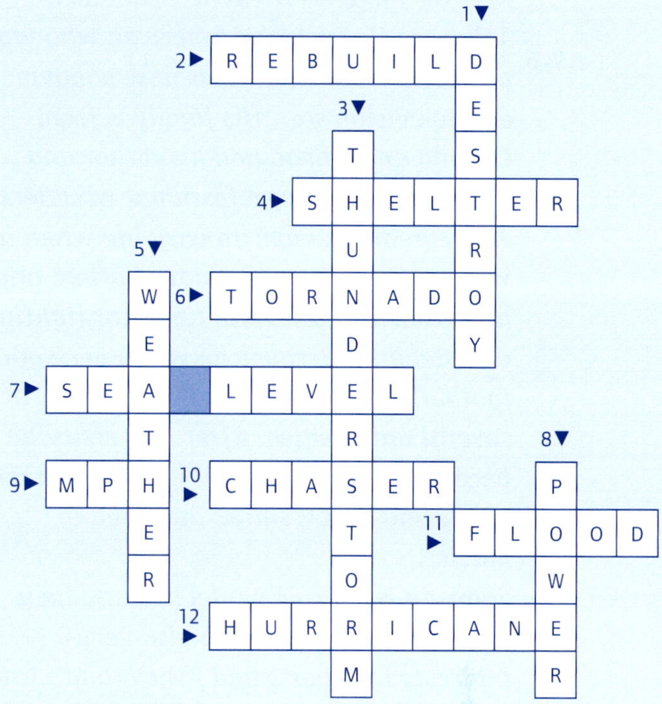

6 SKILLS Building a vocabulary

	Definition/ Translation	Strategy/ Details
1	Make sure/sichern	similar word: sure
2	*Patient*	*similar to German*
3	*Wartezeit*	*word family: to wait*
4	*Personal*	*situation: doctors and nurses*
5	*needing / brauchen*	*word family: to need*
6	*medizinisch*	*situation/ similar to German*
7	*not necessary / unnötig*	*prefix un- + known word necessary*
8	*diagnostizieren*	*similar to German*
9	*eine Art Wunde*	*situation: together with cuts*
10	*Asthma*	*similar to German*
11	*Raumschiff*	*compound word: space + ship*
12	*Themen-*	*similar to German; situation*

7 GUIDED WRITING A scrapbook entry

Mögliche Lösung:

My role model is Dwayne "The Rock" Johnson. He's a black American who was a professional athlete; he is now a movie and television star. His family is from Canada and Samoa and his father and grandfather were professional wrestlers. Johnson didn't have an easy life when he was a child. His family moved often, and he was arrested several times for fighting and stealing. Because he was a very good football player, he was offered places at several universities. After university he became a very famous wrestler. He started appearing on TV shows and then in movies.

Johnson is my role model because he is such a great athlete. I'm also very interested in sports and fitness and I find him really inspiring. He is also a talented actor and he even sings in some movies: I love watching him on screen! In addition, Johnson founded a charity that helps children with illnesses and family problems and supports other charities. I really respect him for this work.

Zur Korrektur und Bewertung der ***Guided-Writing***-Aufgaben s. S. 5 hier in den Lösungen.

8 MEDIATION At the doctor's

Doctor: Guten Tag. Was kann ich für euch tun?

You: Meine Freundin kann leider nicht so gut Deutsch sprechen. Sie ist erst seit ein paar Tagen in Deutschland. ***Sie hat ihre Allergietabletten nicht mitgebracht und braucht welche.*** (2 P)

Doctor: Frag sie bitte, wogegen sie allergisch ist.

You: ***What are you allergic to?*** (1 P)

Friend: Different kinds of trees, grass and cats.

You: ***Sie ist allergisch gegen verschiedene Bäume, Gras und Katzen.*** (1 P)

Doctor: Bekommt sie schwere allergische Reaktionen?

You: ***Are your allergies very bad? / Do you have very bad allergic reactions?*** (1 P)

Friend: No, I just get red eyes and my nose runs. Sometimes I have to sneeze a lot.

You: *Das Wort „sneeze" verstehst du nicht. Frage nach!* ***What does "sneeze" mean?*** (1 P)

Friend: *Spielt Niesen vor.* When you go like this: Achoo!

You: ***Sie bekommt rote Augen und die Nase läuft. Manchmal muss sie ganz viel niesen.*** (2 P)

Doctor: Nimmt sie die Tabletten jeden Tag?

You: ***Do you take the pills every day?*** (1 P)

Friend: No, just when I need them. That's why I didn't bring them: I haven't needed them for a long time.

You: ***Nein, nur nach Bedarf. Sie brauchte sie seit längerer Zeit gar nicht.*** (2 P)

Doctor: Verstehe. Ich stelle ihr ein Rezept aus. Ihr könnt es vorne an der Rezeption abholen.

You: ***He's/She's giving you a prescription. We can get it from the receptionist.*** (2 P)

Friend: Thank you!

You: ***Vielen Dank. Auf Wiedersehen.*** (1 P)

In Canada

Lösungen Schulaufgabe A

1 LISTENING Trip to Churchill

06

Hörtext:

In the school holiday in October my family went to Canada. The best part was when we visited a town called Churchill. Every autumn, polar bears walk through the town on their way to the ice of the Hudson Bay. There are tours that visitors can take to see the bears in the wilderness.

You have to fly or take a train to Churchill because no roads go there. We flew to Winnipeg and then took a short flight to Churchill.

To see the polar bears, you spend the day on a huge bus with very big tyres. There's a kind of balcony at the back of the bus where you can stand and watch the bears from outside. There were 20 people on our bus. You have to dress very warmly: hat, gloves, boots and snow pants.

The trip out to the bay was absolutely amazing! We saw more bears than I could count. Several bears came very close to the vehicle: I took hundreds of great photos. We even saw polar bears enjoying a dinner of fresh seal: a bit disgusting, but fascinating.

Our tour guide Bianca knew everything about the bears and answered all of our questions. Our driver was excellent, and everyone was really friendly.

There was a talk in the hotel at night about how global warming is hurting the bears. There is less ice every year, so the bears have fewer months when they can hunt. That means some of them are really starving … and more likely to attack people.

You can see more of my photos on my blog at www dot keiras hyphen polar hyphen adventure dot example dot com. That's www dot K E I R A S hyphen polar hyphen adventure dot example dot com.

1 Tourists can view polar bears in town and in the ***wilderness / (Hudson) Bay.***

2 You can only get to the town by plane or ***train.***

3 You ride on a ***bus*** to view the polar bears.

4 The tour group had ***20*** members.

5 The tourists watched bears eating a ***seal.***

6 The group learned about the bears from their ***tour guide.***

7 During an evening presentation, the group heard how ***global warming*** is harming the bears.

8 Bears attack people more often if they are ***starving.***

9 There are more pictures at www.***keiras***-polar-adventure.example.com.

USE OF ENGLISH

2 LANGUAGE Questions about the trip

1 ***Isn't Churchill (a little) boring at night?***

2 ***Didn't you do other things in Churchill?***

3 ***Weren't you scared of the polar bears?***

4 ***Hadn't you ever seen polar bears before?***

5 ***Don't the guides have to have guns?***

6 ***Wasn't it crowded on the bus?***

7 ***Couldn't you see other animals from the bus?***

8 ***Isn't it better to spend school holidays on a beach?***

9 ***Wouldn't you like to go back there?***

10 ***Can't you show us/me more photos?***

3 LANGUAGE Planning the trip to Churchill

First, we had to (1) ***do*** some research. I (2) ***made*** the suggestion to go to Churchill because I once (3) ***did*** a project on polar bears. My parents had to (4) ***make*** a lot of phone calls to make the reservations. We started (5) ***making*** plans over a year ago! We (6) ***made*** lots of lists of things to bring with us, places to go and things to (7) ***do***.

4 WORDS Let's go camping

1 *wilderness*
2 *shovel*
3 *autumn*
4 *outdoors, canoeing, fishing*
5 *tent, cabin*
6 *logging*
7 *corn*

5 WORDS Life in Canada

1 Life in the Canadian wilderness can be a real ***adventure.***
2 Most French Canadians are ***descendants*** of French settlers.
3 About half a million Canadians work for the ***mining*** industry.
4 French and English are the ***national*** languages of Canada.
5 Companies need ***permission*** to build mines.
6 ***Legends*** about huge ancient beavers in Canada are true!
7 Scientists have found bones that ***confirm*** the stories.
8 It's a ***relief*** that the huge beavers aren't
9 ***alive*** today: they sound scary!

6 SKILLS Describing visuals

a

1 *B*; **2** *A*; **3** – ; **4** *F*; **5** *C*; **6** *D*, **7** *E*

b

True: ***1, 4, 5, 8***
False: ***2, 7***
Not in the text: ***3, 6***

7 GUIDED WRITING A letter to a magazine

Mögliche Lösung:

Flora Schmidt
Elchweg 42
Munich
19 May, 20XX

Dear Sir or Madam,

I'm writing about an article that appeared in your magazine about using indigenous names for sports teams.

I think that it is wrong for teams to use these names. I believe that they support stereotypes about indigenous peoples, for example that they are all strong and like to fight. This is an old view of indigenous people that has no place in modern culture.

People who want to keep these names often say that they aren't hurting anyone. I disagree: I believe that stereotypes really hurt people. We need to see each other with respect. Some fans argue that these names have been used for many years and are an important part of their team's identity. I can understand that a name is a big part of a team's identity. But I believe that fans can see this change in a positive way.

All in all, I believe that there are no really good reasons for keeping these kind of team names. Let's all try to respect each other's races and cultures.

Yours sincerely,

Flora Schmidt, Munich

Zur Korrektur und Bewertung der ***Guided-Writing***-Aufgaben s. S. 5 hier in den Lösungen.

In Canada

Lösungen Schulaufgabe B

Unit **5**

1 READING Important messages

1 *C*; 2 *B*; 3 *B*; 4 *A*; 5 *B*; 6 *A*; 7 *A*; 8 *C*

USE OF ENGLISH

2 LANGUAGE A weekend in the woods

I ***myself*** was never so wild about the idea of spending a weekend in the woods: Luisa ***herself*** was the one who suggested it. I let ***myself*** be talked into it by her. But I actually enjoyed ***myself*** more than she did!
Luisa's uncle finally brought ***himself*** to a phone and confirmed that we could use his cabin. He'd built it ***himself*** in the wilderness of Ontario.
When we got there, we saw that some animals had made ***themselves*** a home in the bedroom. Luisa was really scared that they would come back, but I'm sure they ***themselves*** were frightened to do that while we were there. I started to clean the room but Luisa excused ***herself***, saying she was allergic to animals. Luisa spent most of the weekend entertaining ***herself*** with her smartphone. I ***myself*** set off for a long walk in the woods each morning. I taught ***myself*** canoeing, went hiking and kept ***myself*** busy with fishing and birdwatching.

3 LANGUAGE Working at the rodeo

You ***have to arrive*** at work on time! If you are ill and ***aren't/won't be able to come*** to work, you ***have to let us know*** as soon as possible. Last year, ticket takers ***didn't have to wear*** a uniform; this year, you ***have to wear*** a uniform. The factory ***wasn't able/hasn't been able to finish*** the uniforms yet, so ***we won't be able to give*** them to you until next week. Starting next week, ticket takers ***will be allowed to buy*** two tickets each week at a lower price for their friends and family. You ***won't be able/allowed to choose*** the seats.

4 WORDS At a rodeo

a

1 ▶	b	r	o	n	c						
	2 ▶	b	a	r	r	e	l				
		3 ▶	b	u	c	k					
4 ▶	c	o	m	p	e	t	i	t	i	o	n
	5 ▶	h	e	l	m	e	t				
		6 ▶	s	t	r	a	p				
7 ▶	r	e	l	a	y						
8 ▶	s	a	d	d	l	e					

b
Some people say that rodeos are a kind of ***cruelty*** to horses.

5 WORDS Going camping

1 *to scare animals*
2 *to sleep in*
3 *to carry things in*
4 *to hunt*
5 *to help you walk*
6 *to eat*
7 *to catch animals*
8 *for light*
9 *to sleep in*
10 *to dig holes*
11 *to go canoeing*
12 *to cut wood*

6 MEDIATION Finding Anne of Green Gables on Prince Edward Island

1 *Vorbild für Avonlea, die Stadt in den Anne-Büchern* (1 P)
2 *Cousine und Cousin waren Vorbilder für Matthew und Marilla: adoptieren Anne in den Büchern / ihr Haus war Vorbild für Green Gables* (2 P)
3 *Haus besichtigen / an Aktivitäten mit Roman-Figuren teilnehmen / Wanderungen zu Orten aus den Büchern* (2 P)
4 *zwei verschiedene Musicals zu Anne ansehen / Souvenirs kaufen / in einer Pferdekutsche fahren / Essen und Trinken wie in den Büchern beschrieben genießen* (3 P)
5 *die Landschaften, die Montgomery in den Büchern beschreibt* (1 P)

7 GUIDED WRITING A special place

Mögliche Lösung:

To:

Subject:

Dear …

I can't wait to see you again! I really want to take you to the lake in our town. It's called … which means … in English. It's about a kilometre from my house and it's really beautiful.

We go there a lot because there's so much to do there. You can go swimming and fishing in the summer and skating in the winter. There's a cafe with really good ice cream. And my friends and I meet there to hang out a lot when the weather is nice.

The lake really means a lot to me because my friends and I spend so much time there.

We've had some big talks lying in the grass together! It's the place where I learned to swim and skate. I caught a fish for the first time there too. And sometimes I just like to take a quiet walk around the lake by myself.

Have a safe trip!

Yours,

Zur Korrektur und Bewertung der ***Guided-Writing***-Aufgaben s. S. 5 hier in den Lösungen.

8 SKILLS Ask an expert

You: ***When did the giant beavers live?*** (1 P)

Expert: The first of Canada's giant beavers, which were herbivores, lived about 30 million years ago.

You: ***What is a herbivore?*** (1 P)

Expert: A herbivore is an animal that only eats plants.

You: ***You mentioned that giant beavers lived about*** 30 million years ago. (1 P) ***When did the last ones die?*** (1 P)

Expert: The last ones died about 10,000 years ago.

You: ***Why did they die?*** (1 P)

Expert: We don't really know why they died. The climate changed then: maybe it wasn't the right climate for them.

You: ***What exactly do you mean by that? / Can you explain a bit more?*** (1 P)

Expert: Well, at that time there were periods of warm weather and then periods of very cold weather. Not all animals survived that change. It also meant that some plants didn't survive. Animals that ate those plants might have starved.

You: ***Where did the giant beavers live?*** (1 P)

Expert: They lived in lakes near swamps.

You: ***How big/long were the giant beavers?*** (1 P)

Expert: The giant beavers were about two and a half metres long.

You: ***Wow!/That's really interesting!*** (1 P) ***How tall were they?*** (1 P)

Expert: They were about one metre tall.

You: ***Can you repeat that?*** (1 P)

Expert: They were about one metre tall.

Arbeitsanweisungen

Viele der in diesem Heft verwendeten Arbeitsanweisungen kennst du aus deinem Schülerbuch.
Die folgenden Arbeitsanweisungen sind möglicherweise neu für dich:

Complete the tasks.	Löse die Aufgaben.
Match the number of each question with the correct answer below.	Ordne die Ziffer jeder Frage der richtigen Antwort unten zu.
Use the word given in capitals at the end of each line to form a word from the same word family that fits in the space on the same line.	Verwende jedes in Großbuchstaben geschriebene Wort am Zeilenende, um eine anderes Wort aus der Wortfamilie zu bilden, das in die Lücke des Satzes passt.
You do not have to fill all spaces, and some information may go in more than one space.	Du musst nicht alle Lücken füllen, und manche Information passt in mehr als eine Lücke.
Read the clues and complete the crossword.	Lies die Hinweise und vervollständige das Kreuzworträtsel.
Number the phrases of the presentation in the right order.	Nummeriere die Sätze der Präsentation in der richtigen Reihenfolge.
Listen to the debate and complete the grid below.	Höre dir die Debatte an und vervollständige die Tabelle unten.
Write words from the same families as the highlighted words.	Schreibe Wörter aus derselben Wortfamilie wie die markierten Wörter.
Make negative questions to go with the answers.	Bilde verneinte Fragen, die zu den Antworten passen.
Ask follow-up questions to find out more.	Stelle Anschlussfragen, um mehr herauszufinden.

Trackliste der Hörverstehensaufgaben

Track	Unit	Buchseite	Titel	Einzellaufzeit
1	**1**	6	**LANGUAGE Writing the date**	0:48
2	**1**	12	**LISTENING Shopping trip**	2:24
3	**2**	23	**LISTENING A school debate**	4:20
4	**3**	35	**LISTENING On the radio**	4:35
5	**4**	38	**LISTENING Stopped by the police**	2:34
6	**5**	53	**LISTENING Trip to Churchill**	2:20

Gesamtlaufzeit der Tonaufnahmen: 17:01

Diese Tabellen sollen dir bei der Bewertung deiner Übungsschulaufgaben helfen.
Deine Lehrerin oder dein Lehrer legt möglicherweise einen anderen Bewertungsmaßstab zugrunde.

Gesamtpunktzahl 66

Note 1	Note 2	Note 3	Note 4	Note 5	Note 6
66 – 58	57 – 50	49 – 41	40 – 33	32 – 21	20 – 0

Gesamtpunktzahl 67

Note 1	Note 2	Note 3	Note 4	Note 5	Note 6
67 – 59	58 – 51	50 – 42	41 – 34	33 – 21	20 – 0

Gesamtpunktzahl 69

Note 1	Note 2	Note 3	Note 4	Note 5	Note 6
69 – 61	60 – 52	51 – 43	42 – 35	34 – 22	21 – 0

Gesamtpunktzahl 74

Note 1	Note 2	Note 3	Note 4	Note 5	Note 6
74 – 66	65 – 56	55 – 46	45 – 36	35 – 24	23 – 0

Gesamtpunktzahl 75

Note 1	Note 2	Note 3	Note 4	Note 5	Note 6
75 – 67	66 – 57	56 – 47	46 – 37	36 – 25	24 – 0

Gesamtpunktzahl 84

Note 1	Note 2	Note 3	Note 4	Note 5	Note 6
84 – 74	73 – 63	62 – 53	52 – 42	41 – 27	26 – 0

Gesamtpunktzahl 87

Note 1	Note 2	Note 3	Note 4	Note 5	Note 6
87 – 77	76 – 66	65 – 55	54 – 44	43 – 28	27 – 0

6 MEDIATION Product review

____/10

Your little sister wants a smartwatch. The one she likes is not sold in Germany yet, but you found a review of it on an American website. Answer her questions.

Cool kids' watch

The two most interesting features of the TimeDog smartwatch are communication and tracking. The watch is sold in black, blue, purple, red, silver and white, meaning that almost everyone will find a color to love. The price is a little higher than other kids' smartwatches, but the quality is better. It makes a great birthday or holiday present.
Our testers loved it and it has lots of other kid-friendly features. Kids really like the way it looks too: not too babyish and very high-tech.
There's a great emergency button[1] that lets kids get help fast. GPS makes sure parents can always find their child. And you can use the watch as a phone, although you do need to buy a SIM card to use these communication features. The battery life is good: at least 24 hours when completely charged. The watch comes with 10 fun games.
One disadvantage of this smartwatch is the camera, which doesn't take great pictures. But there are lots of built-in stickers and effects you can use on your photos and videos.
The watch is very user-friendly: our testers had it working in a couple of minutes. The box is made from recycled materials.

[1]**button** [ˈbʌtn] Knopf

237 users said this review helped them

Sister: Denkst du, diese Rezension ist gut?

You: ____________________, 237 Leute ____. (1 P)

Sister: Kann man mit der Uhr telefonieren?

You: Ja, aber ____. (1 P)

Sister: Können unsere Eltern immer sehen, wo ich bin?

You: ____. (1 P)

Sister: Gibt es die Uhr nur in Rot, wie auf dem Foto?

You: ____. (1 P)

Sister: Warum ist sie so teuer? Andere sind billiger.

You: ____. (1 P)

Sister: Muss man das Ding dauernd aufladen?

You: ____. (1 P)

Sister: Wie ist die Kamera? Kann man Fotos auf der Uhr direkt bearbeiten?

You: ____

____. (3 P)

Sister: Dauert es lange, die Uhr in Betrieb zu nehmen?

You: ____. (1 P)

7 GUIDED WRITING **Car radio advert**

____/15

Write a script for a radio advert for this new car.

Include

- first sentence: very general information (name and brand of the car)
  Introducing / Meet the new ...
- special features of the car
  - how it looks *style · colour*
  - size *room · (to) carry*
  - technical
    electric · pollution · battery · (to) charge
- features
  intelligent technology · seat position · (to) control · built-in · stereo · speaker
- buying information
  (to) offer · (to) order · online

Write 120 words or more.

A changing world

Schulaufgabe B

Unit **3**

Gesamtpunktzahl _____ / 69 Note ____

04

1 LISTENING On the radio

_____ / 7

For each question, tick the correct answer.

1 What kind of volunteer work does this star usually do?

A
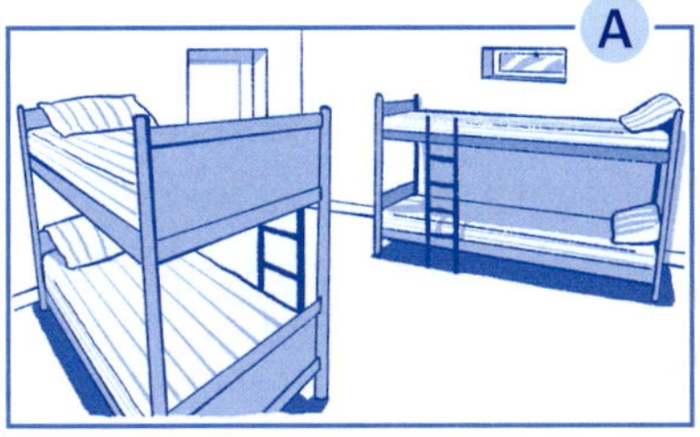

B

C

2 Why is the player moving to Detroit?

A

B

C

3 What did the first caller win?

A

B

C

4 Which of these virtual experiences can you do in a group?

A

B

C

5 What's causing new problems in the cars?

A

B

C

6 Why can't you drive over the bridge?

A

B
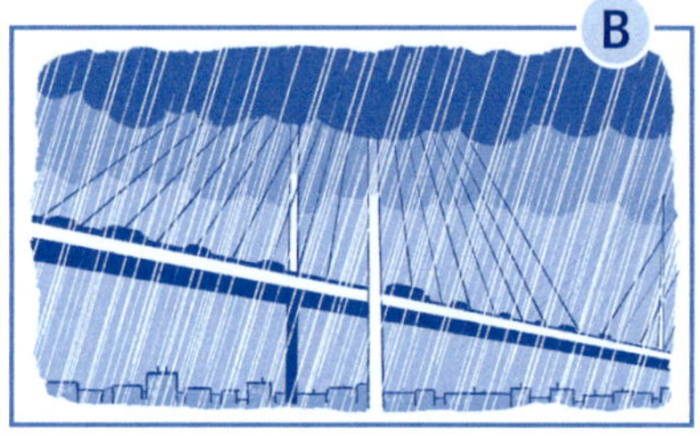
C

7 What does the weatherwoman recommend doing today?

A

B

C

USE OF ENGLISH

2 LANGUAGE Product review: Smart pillow ____/9

Complete the product review with the *passive* (*simple past* or *simple present*) forms of the verbs.

This pillow 1 ____________________ *(give)* to me as a birthday present last week. A lot of features 2 ____________________ *(include)* and some of them are very useful. Your sleep 3 ____________________ *(track)* by sensors in the pillow: you 4 ____________________ *(tell)* every morning how long you have slept. However, my head 5 ____________________ *(not always recognize)* by the pillow, so this feature doesn't work every night.

On the first night I used it, I 6 ____________________ *(wake up)* by music in the middle of the night: the pillow 7 ____________________ *(switch on)* by the app accidentally!

8 I ____________________ *(remind)* every night by the pillow to switch off the light, which is very helpful: I sometimes read in bed for hours and forget to sleep.

And 9 I ____________________ *(prevent)* from sleeping too long by the pillow's alarm!

3 LANGUAGE Visiting national parks

____/7

Choose a verb from the box and complete the sentences about national parks with the correct *participles*. There are three verbs which you don't need.

(to) climb · (to) grow · (to) improve · (to) last · (to) play · (to) reduce · (to) take part · (to) threaten · (to) track · (to) volunteer

1 Climate change is warming up the planet, ________________ our national parks.

2 ________________ dead, a hiker survived an attack by a bear last year.

3 When ________________, Max tells visitors about the wolves in the park.

4 While ________________ to the top of the mountain, I stopped to look at the view.

5 ________________ to over 107 meters high, redwood trees are found in California and Oregon.

6 ________________ animals, scientists find out more about the effects of climate change on their environment.

7 ________________ in extreme sports, some visitors have accidents in national parks.

4 WORDS Say it in English

____/5

Wie sagst/fragst du auf Englisch, …

1 dass deine Tante am Fließband in der Autofabrik arbeitet?

____

2 dass dein Autositz zu weit weg vom Lenkrad ist?

____

3 ob deine Freundin Musik über Kopfhörer oder Lautsprecher hören möchte?

____

4 dass eine neue Erfindung Autounfälle um 10% reduzieren könnte?

____

5 ob dein Freund sein Haus mit seinem Smartphone aufschließen kann.

____

5 WORDS Two meanings

____/8

How is each marked word used? Circle the verbs and underline the nouns.

Example: Seat yourself on the seat.

1 Shelby bought some purple **paint** to **paint** her car purple.

2 That broken **lock** won't **lock** your bike.

3 Our car **features** some of the newest smart **features**.

4 They **track** deer with this device while walking on the **track**.

5 Sometimes we know what **causes** accidents and sometimes we can't find any **causes**.

6 The police said his **speed** was over 100 miles an hour, but he usually doesn't **speed**.

7 She likes to talk with the other **volunteers** when she **volunteers** at the park.

8 I can **repair** it, but the **repair** probably won't last long.

6 SKILLS A review of Henry Ford Museum of American Innovation

____/7

Read the review and the feedback. Give an example, reason or comment for each point in the feedback.

Plan a couple of days for this great experience!

★★★★★

I visited the museum with my family and thought it was AMAZING! There is so much to see and do.
A very big collection of vehicles include the bus Rosa Parks rode in and an exhibition on civil rights to go with it. The car in which President Kennedy was shot can also be seen. There are lots of old trains and even plains from the 1920s to the 1980s. There's also a funny vehicle that looks like a hotdog! My favorite exhibition was the one showing how our lives were changed by the invention of cars. There were also interesting exhibitions about math and even Star Trek!
Be prepared to do a lot of walking! If you need a brake, go into the movie theater and see a film on their extremely big screen.
If you have more than one day, go to the village and experience 300 years of American history or take the factory tour. Even the food was cool! You can have milkshakes at a 1950s restaurant or go to the Michigan Café, where all the food is local.

Is the review easy to understand? ☻	______
Is there enough information? ☻	______ ______
Is the opinion of the writer clear? ☻	______
Does the writer use different adjectives? ☻	(Give at least three examples.) ______ ______
Are the ideas joined with linking words? ☹	(Give at least one suggestion.) ______ ______ ______ ______
Is the grammar correct? 😐	______ ______
Are the spelling and punctuation correct? ☹	(Give at least two examples.) ______ ______

7 MEDIATION Visiting a national park ____/11

Your family has just arrived at Pictured Rocks, one of Michigan's national parks. Your father is busy with your little brother and asks you to find out some information from a park ranger. Use your notes on your conversation to answer your father's questions.

- *Landscapes: beaches, waterfalls, forests, swamps. Pictured Rocks: very tall rocks on the beach, beautiful forms and colours (stripes!)*
- *Wildlife: see small animals and birds. Also deer, bears, wolves, fish*
- *Activities: hiking, walks with rangers, fishing, rent a boat, bird watching, hang out at beach, look at stars at night*
- *Good hikes for kids: Munising Falls trail, hike to Mosquito Beach*
- *Camping: three places to camp, need to book!*

Vater: Also, was sind diese *pictured rocks*? Und wo finden wir sie?

Du: ______________________________

______________________________ (2 P)

Vater: Da müssen wir unbedingt hin! Was gibt es sonst hier für Landschaften?

Du: (give three examples) ______________________________ (1 P)

Vater: Kann man hier mit Kindern gut wandern?

Du: ______________________________

______________________________ (2 P)

Vater: Prima. Was kann man noch alles im Park unternehmen?

Du: (give three examples) ______________________________

____

____

______________________________ (3 P)

Vater: Und was für Tiere gibt es hier?

Du: ______________________________

______________________________ (2 P)

Vater: Hier gibt's offenbar viel zu sehen und zu tun! Kann man hier auch zelten?

Du: ______________________________ (1 P)

Vater: Das wusste ich nicht. Schade!

8 GUIDED WRITING Product review

____/15

Write a review of a drone you bought last week.
Write the text in your exercise book.
Include

- reasons why you bought the drone
- what you like about it
- what you don't like about it

Find a good heading for your review.
Write 120 words or more.
These words and phrases can help you:

air · battery · (to) charge · (to) connect · connection · (to) crash · (dis)advantage · (to) fly · (to) install · (to) last · overall · price · (to) send · (to) take a picture/video · (to) work

Black lives

Schulaufgabe A

Unit **4**

Gesamtpunktzahl _____ / 75   Note ____

1 READING Beyoncé Knowles

_____ / 15

Read the biography of Beyoncé Knowles.

A Beyoncé Giselle Knowles was born in Houston, Texas, on September 4, 1981. The proud parents were Celestine and Mathew Knowles: a hairdresser and a manager. Beyoncé's name comes from her mother's last name Beyincé. Beyoncé has a younger sister, Solange, who she later sang with in the group Destiny's Child. Even as a young girl Beyoncé loved to sing and dance, winning several talent shows. She also sang at her church. At the age of eight she joined a singing group. Her father later became the manager of the group.

B Beyoncé began her education at St. Mary's Montessori School in Houston, where she got people's attention with her dancing. She then moved to Parker Elementary School, which concentrates on music. She performed with the school choir there.

She later went to the High School for the Performing and Visual Arts and then to Alief Elsik High School. However, she didn't graduate from high school because she dropped out to tour with her singing group.

C The group changed its name and members several times, but in 1997 (when Beyoncé was just 16 years old) they made their first album as Destiny's Child. Their second album made them stars with hits like *Say My Name*. They went on to make three more albums together.

In addition to singing, Beyoncé began working as an actor, appearing in films such as *Dreamgirls*. In 2003, Beyoncé made the album *Dangerously in Love* without Destiny's Child. It was a huge success, selling millions of copies and winning five Grammy Awards. She made one more album with Destiny's Child in 2004.

Beyoncé has made six albums alone and one with her husband, the musician Jay-Z. She has sold over 100 million albums, making her one of the world's best-selling singers, and won 22 Grammys.

D In addition to singing and acting, Beyoncé has started several companies, including two lines of fashion. She has also worked as a model for other brands.

Beyoncé has her own media company, which makes music, films and more. She and her husband also own a music streaming service together with other artists.

In 2014, Beyoncé became the highest-paid African-American musician in history. Experts say that she and her husband are the first billion-dollar couple in the music industry.

E Beyoncé has often used her music to raise awareness of causes important to her, such as the *Black Lives Matter* movement. A film she made includes the mothers of Eric Garner, Michael Brown and Trayvon Martin, all victims of police shootings. In 2016 she performed at a concert for Hillary Clinton, who was trying to become America's first female president. She has called herself a feminist and supports LGBT rights. Beyoncé has also worked for stronger gun control laws.

F Beyoncé is the wife of musician Jay-Z, who she married in 2008. Their first child, daughter Blue Ivy Carter, was born in 2012. In 2017 the family grew to include twins: a boy and girl named Sir and Rumi. The family has homes in New York, California and New Orleans.

a Which of the headings (0–7) matches the paragraphs of the text (A–F) best? Write the correct numbers in the boxes. One heading (0) has already been put in the correct place. Use each number only once. Be careful: there are some headings that you do not need to use. ____/5

A ☐ Lines 2–9
B ☐ Lines 10–15
C ☐ Lines 16–25
D ☐ Lines 26–31
E [0] Lines 32–36
F ☐ Lines 37–39

0 Activist
1 Businesswoman
2 Growing up
3 Education
4 Family
5 Famous friends
6 Hobbies
7 Musical career

b Are sentences 1–10 'true' (T) or 'false' (F)? Choose 'not in the text' (N) if there is not enough information to answer 'true' or 'false'. Tick (✓) the correct answer. ____/10

	T	F	N
1 Beyoncé was named after her mother.	☐	☐	☐
2 Solange and Beyoncé spend a lot of time together today.	☐	☐	☐
3 Beyoncé was an excellent student.	☐	☐	☐
4 Beyoncé left school because her musical talents weren't supported there.	☐	☐	☐
5 Beyoncé only became a star after she left Destiny's Child.	☐	☐	☐
6 Beyoncé has won Grammys both alone and with Destiny's Child.	☐	☐	☐
7 Her fashion lines have been Beyoncé's most successful companies.	☐	☐	☐
8 Together, Beyoncé and her husband have earned more than any other married musicians.	☐	☐	☐
9 Beyoncé supports gun rights.	☐	☐	☐
10 Beyoncé and her husband have two daughters and son.	☐	☐	☐

USE OF ENGLISH

2 **LANGUAGE** ***Black Lives Matter*** ____/9

Erin and Luke are preparing a presentation. Put the sentences in the right order.

1 to / the reasons for the movement / We can explain / the class

____

2 some pictures of protest marches / Let's show / them / to

____

3 to / suggested / Our teacher / this book / me

____

4 the story of Trayvon Martin / everyone / Should we tell

______________________________?

5 the class / for their opinion about the movement / We can ask

____

6 you / I'll send / tomorrow / my slides

____

7 them / on Monday / this weekend and / Please look for photos / give / to me

____

8 didn't report / Our town's newspaper / to its readers / this story

____

9 introduce / to / Can you / the topic / the class

______________________________?

3 LANGUAGE After Hurricane Katrina ____/7

Complete Tom's email to his friend with the *personal passive* of the *simple past*.

Dear Luisa,

I ____________ finally ____________ *(allow)* time to use the computer here! We're in a shelter in Texas: we ____________ *(give)* space here after we had left New Orleans. We've been here for a week now. My mother ____________ *(send)* money by friends and relatives, so I ____________ *(buy)* some new clothes yesterday. We're leaving here tomorrow: my parents ____________ *(offer)* an apartment near New Orleans by a friend. I'm happy you're also OK. I ____________ *(show)* the e-mail your mother wrote to my mother.

I ____________ *(ask)* by my mother to say she'll answer soon.

Stay safe!

Tom

4 WORDS Blacks in the U.S. ____/10

Write the letter of the correct word for each gap.

Blacks in the U.S. have fought against **1** ______________ for hundreds of years. The **2** ______________ freed African-Americans from **3** ______________ but **4** ______________ in the south stopped them from getting the same **5** ______________ and using the same facilities as whites. Even worse: unfair laws were **6** ______________ which **7** ______________ African-Americans from voting. The Civil Rights Act of 1964 made discrimination illegal. But even today African-Americans are **8** ______________ of **9** ______________: they are stopped more often than whites by the police because of their **10** ______________.

1	A discrimination	B condition	C registration	D mediation
2	A Civil Rights Act	B movement	C Civil War	D citizenship
3	A reservations	B poverty	C prison	D slavery
4	A organization	B situation	C segregation	D mediation
5	A schools	B education	C learning	D awareness
6	A passed	B sent	C suggested	D parted
7	A charged	B prevented	C destroyed	D pushed
8	A activists	B graduates	C victims	D people
9	A proofing	B proving	C protesting	D profiling
10	A race	B crime	C reaction	D behaviour

5 WORDS Word families: Sport

____/8

Write words from the same families as the highlighted words.

1 ______________________________ are people who do gymnastics.

2 Talented people work hard to develop their ______________________________.

3 The players were ______________________________ awards.

4 The medalists wore their ______________________________ proudly.

5 I was in a lot of ______________________________ from my painful injuries.

6 The boxers were ______________________________ in the ring.

7 The coaches ______________________________ the athletes every day.

8 Who was the champion of the last ______________________________?

6 GUIDED WRITING What's important to me

____/15

People from all over the world have been writing posts about what's important to them on a social media site you use. Write your own post about what's important to you.
Write the text in your exercise book.

Include the following information:

- a description of a thing, person or value that is important to you
- why it/she/he is important to you
- the role of this thing/person/value in your life

Find a suitable beginning and ending. Write about 150 words in your exercise book.

LERNTIPP

- Wähle am besten ein Thema, zu dem du möglichst viel auf Englisch schreiben kannst.
- Diese Aufgabe ist etwas knifflig, weil du sehr viel über eine Person / eine Sache / eine Wertvorstellung schreiben musst. Um ständige Wiederholungen des gleichen Wortes zu vermeiden, suche nach Synonymen, Umschreibungen oder Oberbegriffen. Wenn du z. B. über einen Ring schreibst, kannst du ihn auch als ein *piece of jewellery*, *a band*, *a circle of gold*, *a treasure*, usw. bezeichnen.

7 MEDIATION Calling the doctor's office ___/11

Du bist mit deiner Familie in den USA. Dein Bruder ist krank. Rufe für deine Eltern in einer Arztpraxis an und vereinbare einen Termin für deinen Bruder.

Receptionist: Dr. Weingast's office. How can I help you?

You: ____ (1 P)

Receptionist: Is the appointment for you or for someone else?

You: ____ (1 P)

Receptionist: Can you please give me his name and date of birth?

You: ____ (1 P)

Receptionist: And what's the reason for the appointment?

You: *(Frag deinen Vater, was deinem Bruder fehlt)* ____________________

____ (1 P)

Father: Sein Bauch tut weh und er hat Fieber.

You: ____ (1 P)

Receptionist: I have an appointment free in 45 minutes. Can you get here that quickly?

You: ____

____ (2 P)

Mother: Das wird knapp. Ist das der einzige freie Termin?

You: ____ (1 P)

Receptionist: Yes, I'm sorry.

You: Ja.

Father: Sag ihr, wir sind in einer Dreiviertelstunde da.

You: ____ (1 P)

Receptionist: Does your brother have health insurance?

You: ____ (1 P)

Mother: Ja, hat er.

You: ____ (1 P)

Receptionist: Great. Please bring the documents with you. Goodbye.

You: Thank you. Goodbye.

Black lives

Schulaufgabe B

Unit 4

Gesamtpunktzahl _____/84 Note ____

05 **1 LISTENING Stopped by the police** _____/6

You will hear a conversation with three girls and a police officer. One ending to each of the following sentences (1–6) is correct. Tick (✓) A, B, C or D. You may listen to the conversation twice and take five seconds to complete the task after each listening.

1 Clarissa's friend tells her to …

A ☐ switch off the music.
B ☐ touch the dashboard.
C ☐ hold the steering wheel.
D ☐ switch on her lights.

2 Clarissa and her friends …

A ☐ are going to the library.
B ☐ were at the library.
C ☐ just had some pizza.
D ☐ drove Clarissa's father home.

3 The girls drove …

A ☐ down a street without any houses.
B ☐ through the town very slowly.
C ☐ away from the library shortly before they were stopped.
D ☐ around with some boys in the car.

4 The police officer stopped them …

A ☐ because their car looked like one that was driving suspiciously slowly.
B ☐ for driving too fast through the town.
C ☐ for driving without lights.
D ☐ because a neighborhood watchman said that their music was too loud.

5 The watchman was suspicious because …

A ☐ there were boys in the car.
B ☐ the girls weren't really at the library.
C ☐ the victims asked for help.
D ☐ there had been several crimes in that area recently.

6 The girls knew how to behave because …

A ☐ they're often stopped by the police.
B ☐ they watch a lot of TV.
C ☐ a police officer had visited their school.
D ☐ Oona told them.

LERNTIPP

Wörter aus fast allen Antwortmöglichkeiten kommen im Hörtext vor, aber nur eine Antwort passt genau zum jeweiligen Satzanfang.

USE OF ENGLISH

2 LANGUAGE What would have happened?

____/9

Complete the type 3 *if*-sentences.

1 If Clarissa hadn't been playing music so loudly, ______________________________

______________________________ . *(hear • the police car earlier)*

2 The girls would have left the library earlier ______________________ . *(get hungry)*

3 ______________________________ if it hadn't been the same kind as the other car. *(police officer • not stop • Clarissa's car)*

4 Clarissa and her father could have gotten to the library earlier ______________________

______________________________ . *(not go to her friends' houses)*

5 ______________________________ if there hadn't been burglars in the neighborhood recently. *(watchman • not be suspicious)*

6 ______________________________ if they had been the burglars. *(police officer • arrest • girls)*

7 The girls wouldn't have known how to behave ______________________________

______________________________ . *(police officer • not visit • their school)*

8 Clarissa would have remembered to put her hands on the wheel ______________________

______________________________ . *(not be • so nervous)*

9 ______________________________ if you had been driving the car? *(you • be nervous)*

3 LANGUAGE Marques had a hard day

____/9

Write the correct ending for each word: *-ed* or *-ing*.

1 School was really challeng________ but not especially inspir________ .

2 After school, he had baseball practice, which was extremely tir________ .

3 His baseball coach is pretty relax________ , but his teammates aren't.

4 Marques is worri________ about a test tomorrow. His last grade was disappoint________ .

5 He's also embarrass________ about something stupid he said in class.

6 It's not supris________ that he's going to bed early. He'll feel energiz________ in the morning.

4 WORDS Slavery in the United States ____/8

Answer the questions. You do not have to write complete sentences. The words in the box may help you. You may not need all of the words in the box. You can use words more than one time.

Africa · ban · Civil War · discrimination · escape · field · free · north · south · states · task

1 From which continent were slaves brought to the United States? ____________

2 What type of work did most slaves do? ____________

3 In what part of the U.S. did most slaves live? ____________

4 What did Harriet Tubman help other slaves to do? ____________

5 What war started in the U.S. in 1861? ____________

6 What were the two sides in the war? ____________

7 Who won the war? ____________

8 What did Abraham Lincoln do about slavery? ____________

5 WORDS Storms ____/11

Complete the crossword puzzle.

1 to damage sth. so badly that it doesn't exist any more: hurricanes and tornados can do this
2 to create something again: people did this in New Orleans after Katrina, especially to houses
3 a type of very bad weather with loud noises
4 a place where you can stay when you don't have a home
5 you can describe this with adjectives like rainy, windy, sunny …
6 a dangerous storm with extremely strong winds that move in a circle
7 a lot of New Orleans is below this point (two words)
8 electricity
9 an abbreviation for talking about how fast sth. moves
10 a person who goes to places where there are big storms
11 when a lot of water covers an area that's usually dry
12 Katrina was one of these

6 SKILLS Building your vocabulary ____/ 12

You are visiting New Orleans and your little sister needs a doctor. Read this website. There are some words you don't know. For each highlighted word, give a definition or translation and write the strategy you used to find the meaning. Give details: for example, related words you used.

Kid Care New Orleans

KCNO's mission is to **1 ensure** our young **2 patients** get excellent care without long **3 waits**. Our **4 staff** is made up of emergency doctors and nurses who are specially trained in helping children **5 in need of** quick, professional care. Our aim is to give fast **6 medical** attention without **7 unnecessary** pain and tests.

We **8 diagnose** and treat conditions including:

- cuts and **9 scrapes**
- broken bones
- high temperature
- pain
- infections
- **10 asthma**

We provide your insurance company or doctor with reports, diagnoses and test results.

We're there when you need us

- We are open 24 hours a day, 365 days a year.
- Most insurance plans accepted.
- We are proud of our clean, child-friendly facilities.

Each room has a different design:
our young patients love our magic castle, **11 spaceship**, jungle and other **12 theme** rooms.

	Definition/ Translation	Strategy/ Details		Definition/ Translation	Strategy/ Details
1	*make sure / sichern*	*similar word: sure*	2	______ ______ ______	______ ______ ______
3	______ ______ ______	______ ______ ______	4	______ ______ ______	______ ______ ______

	Definition/ Translation	Strategy/ Details		Definition/ Translation	Strategy/ Details
5	______ ______ ______	______ ______ ______	6	______ ______ ______	______ ______ ______
7	______ ______ ______	______ ______ ______	8	______ ______ ______	______ ______ ______
9	______ ______ ______	______ ______ ______	10	______ ______ ______	______ ______ ______
11	______ ______ ______	______ ______ ______	12	______ ______ ______	______ ______ ______

7 GUIDED WRITING A scrapbook entry ____/15

Your class is making a scrapbook about your role models. You can write about a famous person or someone you know.

Write your entry and describe

- the person
- what he or she has done
- why he or she is your role model

Write about 120 words in your exercise book.

LERNTIPP

Versuche hier Wiederholungen zu vermeiden. Trenne also die Person von ihren Leistungen. Beim ersten Punkt erzählst du eher über den Hintergrund der Person (Nationalität, Job, Alter …). Beim zweiten Punkt geht es um das Besondere an der Person: *She/He was the first/only/best …* Dann geht es darum, was du persönlich an der Person so toll findest: Warum spricht er/sie dich an?

8 **MEDIATION** **At the doctor's** ____/ 14

You have an American exchange student visiting you. She needs a prescription for her allergy pills. Complete the conversation at the doctor's office.

Doctor: Guten Tag. Was kann ich für euch tun?

You: Meine Freundin kann leider nicht so gut Deutsch sprechen: Sie ist erst seit ein paar Tagen in Deutschland. ____________________

____________________ (2 P)

Doctor: Frag sie bitte, wogegen sie allergisch ist.

You: ____________________ (1 P)

Friend: Different kinds of trees, grass and cats.

You: ____________________ (1 P)

Doctor: Bekommt sie schwere allergische Reaktionen?

You: ____________________ (1 P)

Friend: No, I just get red eyes and my nose runs. Sometimes I have to sneeze a lot.

You: *Das Wort „sneeze" verstehst du nicht. Frage nach!* ____________________ (1 P)

Friend: *Spielt Niesen vor.* When you go like this: Achoo!

You: ____________________

____________________ (2 P)

Doctor: Nimmt sie die Tabletten jeden Tag?

You: ____________________ (1 P)

Friend: No, just when I need them. That's why I didn't bring them: I haven't needed them for a long time.

You: ____________________

____________________ (2 P)

Doctor: Verstehe. Ich stelle ihr ein Rezept aus. Ihr könnt es vorne an der Rezeption abholen.

You: ____________________

____________________ (2 P)

Friend: Thank you!

You: ____________________ (1 P)

In Canada

Schulaufgabe A

Unit 5

Gesamtpunktzahl _____ /74 Note ____

06 **1** **LISTENING** **Trip to Churchill** ____ /9

You will hear a girl giving a presentation about a trip she took to Churchill, Canada. Write the correct answer in each gap: one or two words, a number, a date or a time.

1 Tourists can view polar bears in town and in the ____________________.

2 You can only get to the town by plane or ____________.

3 You ride on a ____________ to view the polar bears.

4 The tour group had ____________________ members.

5 The tourists watched bears eating a ____________________.

6 The group learned about the bears from their ____________ ____________.

7 During an evening presentation, the group heard how ____________ ____________ is harming the bears.

8 Bears attack people more often if they are ____________________.

9 There are more pictures at www.____________________-polar-adventure.example.com.

LERNTIPP

In Aufgaben wie dieser werden die Lückensätze meistens anders formuliert als die entsprechenden Sätze in dem dazu gehörenden Hörtext. Achte deshalb auf Synonyme und Umschreibungen der Aussagen der Lückensätze. Die Wörter, die du in die Lücken schreiben sollst, sind aber immer identisch mit Wörtern aus dem Hörtext.

Beispiel:

Lückensatz: A night at the best _hotel_ in the city is extremely expensive.

Hörtextauszug: It costs a lot of money to stay at the city's top hotel.

2 LANGUAGE Questions about the trip

____/10

Make negative questions about the trip to go with the answers.

1 ______________________________

No, Churchill isn't boring at night: there's always something to do at the hotel.

2 ______________________________

Yes, we did do other things in Churchill: we went to the information centre.

3 ______________________________

No, I wasn't scared of the polar bears: we were on the bus.

4 ______________________________

Yes, I had seen polar bears before, but only in a zoo.

5 ______________________________

Yes, the guides have to have guns, but they never use them.

6 ______________________________

No, it wasn't crowded on the bus: there was enough room for everyone.

7 ______________________________

Yes, we could see other animals from the bus, but the bears were the most interesting.

8 ______________________________

No, it isn't better to spend school holidays on a beach: I love cold weather.

9 ______________________________ Yes, I would like to go back there!

10 ______________________________ Yes, I can show you more photos.

3 LANGUAGE Planning the trip to Churchill

____/7

Complete the gaps with the correct form of *make* or *do*.

First, we had to (1) ____________ some research. I (2) ____________ the suggestion to go to Churchill because I once (3) ____________ a project on polar bears. My parents had to (4) ____________ a lot of phone calls to make the reservations. We started (5) ____________ plans over a year ago! We (6) ____________ lots of lists of things to bring with us, places to go and things to (7) ____________.

4 WORDS Let's go camping

___/10

Find the right words to describe your plans for a camping trip.

1 We're going to camp in *(a place far away from towns and roads)* the ____________________

2 I'll bring a *(piece of equipment)* ____________________ to dig a hole for a toilet.

3 My friend would like to go in *(the season between summer and winter)* this ____________________ , before it gets too cold.

4 I love being *(not inside)* ____________________ and doing activities like *(going out on the water in a light boat)* ____________________ and *(putting a line in the water and catching animals with it)* ____________________ .

5 Camping means sleeping in *(a shelter made of strong cloth)* a ____________________ , not in a *(small house made of wood)* ____________________ .

6 *(An industry that cuts down trees for wood and paper)* ____________________ is a big industry in Canada, but there are still lots of forests where you can go camping.

7 Nothing tastes better than *(a long yellow vegetable with lots of small pieces)* ____________________ cooked over a fire!

5 WORDS Life in Canada

___/9

Use the word given in capitals at the end of each line to form a word from the same word family that fits in the space on the same line.

1	Life in the Canadian wilderness can be a real ____________________ .	ADVENTUROUS
2	Most French Canadians are ____________________ of French settlers.	DESCEND
3	About half a million Canadians work for the ______________ industry.	MINER
4	French and English are the ____________________ languages of Canada.	NATION
5	Companies need ____________________ to build mines.	PERMIT
6	____________________ about huge ancient beavers in Canada are true!	LEGENDARY
7	Scientists have found bones that ____________________ the stories.	CONFIRMATION
8	It's a ____________________ that the huge beavers aren't	RELIEVED
9	____________________ today: they sound scary!	LIFE

6 **SKILLS** **Describing visuals** ___/14

a Write the letter of each type of visual in the correct box. ___/6

A map **B** infographic **C** bar chart **D** line chart **E** Venn diagram **F** pie chart

1 ◯

2 ◯

3

4 ◯

5 ◯

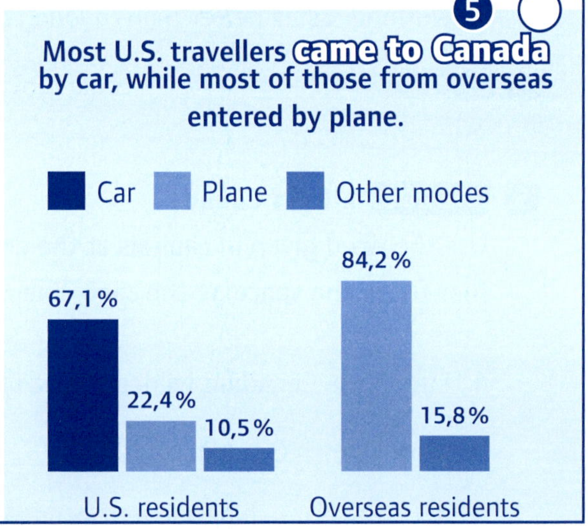

Sources: Infographics 1–5: Statistics Canada, Frontier Counts; Visitor Travel Survey (preliminary)

6 ◯

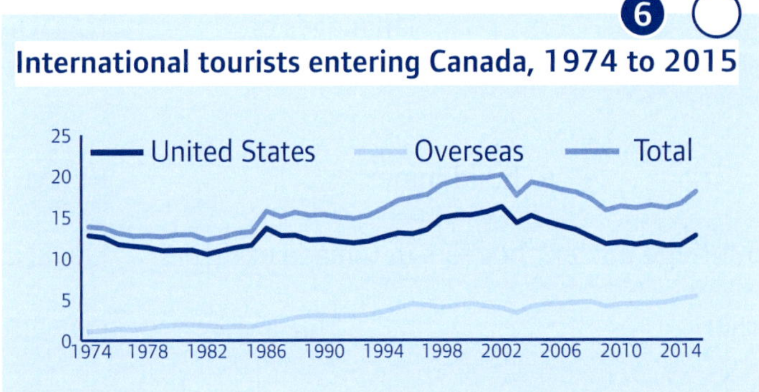

Source: Statistics Canada, CANSIM table 4270004 and Travel Between Canada and Other Countries

7 ◯

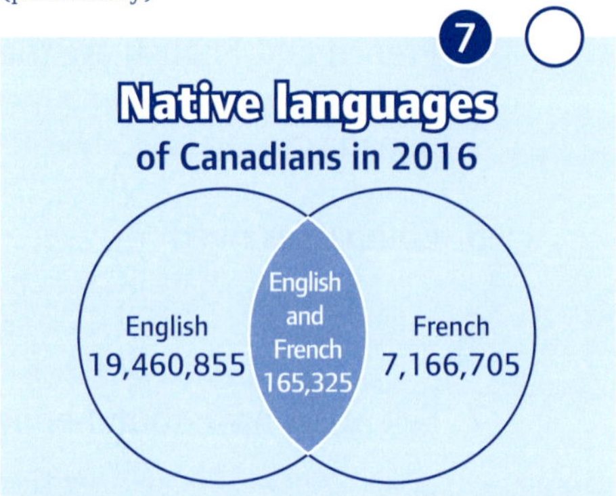

Source: Statistics Canada, Language Highlight Tables, 2016 Census

[1]**percentage** [pəˈsentɪdʒ] Prozentsatz [2]**overseas** Übersee [3]**resident** [ˈrezɪdənt] Bewohner/in

b Is the information below true (T), false (F) or not in one of the visuals on page 56 (N)? Tick (√) the correct box.

____/8

	T	F	N
1 People who live in other countries spent more than $11 billion in Canada in 2018.	☐	☐	☐
2 In 2018, tourists spent more money on food and drink than for places to stay.	☐	☐	☐
3 No one from Japan visited Canada in 2018.	☐	☐	☐
4 More people in Canada speak English as a native language than French.	☐	☐	☐
5 In 2002, the number of US tourists visiting Canada rose to about 14 million but then fell the next year.	☐	☐	☐
6 417,000 Germans flew to Canada in 2018.	☐	☐	☐
7 Visitors to Canada only went to Ontario, British Columbia and Quebec in 2018.	☐	☐	☐
8 In 2018, most international visitors to Canada got there by plane.	☐	☐	☐

7 GUIDED WRITING A letter to a magazine

____/15

You have read an article in a magazine about sports teams in Canada and the US that have names and symbols connected with indigenous peoples, often in a negative way, such as the Eskimos, the Chiefs or the Redskins. Below are your notes about the reasons for and against using these names.

For
- *names don't really mean anything: used so long that no one thinks about meaning*
- *changing names hurts teams' identities*
- *OK if used respectfully*

Against
- *shouldn't be used if indigenous people have protested: they should decide*
- *names support negative stereotypes of indigenous people*
- *wouldn't be OK to use names of other races as team names*

What's your opinion about these names? Should they be used?
Write a letter to the editor. Include the following aspects:
- why you are writing
- your opinion
- arguments against the opposite opinion
- a summary of your position

Find a suitable beginning and ending. Write about 150 words.
Write the text in your exercise book.

LERNTIPP

Auf S. 88 und 161 in deinem Schülerbuch findest du mehr Hilfe zum Verfassen eines Leserbriefs und zum Aufbau eines Briefs.

Unit 5

In Canada

Schulaufgabe B

Gesamtpunktzahl _____/84 Note ____

1 **READING** **Important messages** ____/8

What does each message say? Tick the correct answer.

1

POLAR BEAR AREA

Polar bears can be in town at any time! Stay near your vehicle or other shelter and travel in groups. Don't go out after 10 pm. Never get near or feed bears.

A ☐ There are always some polar bears in town.

B ☐ Always travel by car.

C ☐ You shouldn't walk around at night.

2

Although our bus is heated inside, watching the bears from the outdoor balcony is one of the most exciting parts of the tour. If you need more warm clothes, please see the list of area shops below: there are no extra clothes on the bus.

A ☐ There are extra warm clothes are on the bus.

B ☐ You can buy warm clothes locally.

C ☐ The balcony where you can watch the bears is heated.

3

Mom,

You seemed so tired that Dad and I decided to let you sleep! You can get breakfast downstairs until 11 am. We'll be at the visitor centre until about 12 and we'll come back about half an hour later. Join us if you can!

Frank

A ☐ Frank's mother didn't want to go the visitor centre.

B ☐ Frank and his father will be back from the visitor centre at about 12:30.

C ☐ Frank's mother should eat breakfast at 11 am.

4

Zoe,
I haven't been able to reach my uncle to ask about using his cabin from Friday to Sunday. Any other ideas for a place to stay? I've really been looking forward to a few days of hiking and fishing: I hope we can still go!
Luisa

Luisa is writing to Zoe

A ☐ for suggestions about where else they could spend the weekend.

B ☐ to say how excited she is about their trip.

C ☐ to say that they can use her uncle's cabin.

5

Arlington Bicycle Rodeo

Everyone taking part in the rodeo must wear a helmet and use the strap. Please speak to one of the officers if you need help with your helmet. We have a few helmets to lend to riders at the information desk.

A ☐ Everyone has to have a helmet on while on their horse.

B ☐ The police can check your helmet.

C ☐ Everyone can get a helmet at the information desk.

6

The starting time of today's relay race has been moved up to 1 pm because of the storm in the late afternoon. Please check your mail: changing weather conditions may cause us to cancel the event at the last minute.

A ☐ The relay race may not take place.

B ☐ The race will now take place later than planned.

C ☐ The race has been cancelled because of a storm.

7

RODEO WORKERS NEEDED

We are looking for ticket takers for our weekend events. Great job for students! Hours are Saturdays between 10 am and 2 pm. Must stand outside in all weather.

Only apply for this job if

A ☐ you will work outdoors in different conditions.

B ☐ you are a student.

C ☐ you enjoy riding horses.

8

Eric,
Let me know if you need help with your homework. I'll have time at about 8 pm. I'll leave work at 5:30, then go to the supermarket. You can start washing and cutting potatoes at about 6:15.
Dad

A ☐ Eric has to cook dinner at 6:15.

B ☐ Eric's father will be at the supermarket at 5:30.

C ☐ Eric should tell his father whether he should work with him on tasks for school tonight.

LERNTIPP

Hier geht es darum, die wichtigsten Aspekte von Mitteilungen zu erkennen. Vergleiche jede der drei Antwortmöglichkeiten mit dem Text, bevor du dich für eine entscheidest. Prüfe noch einmal: Passt wirklich alles im Text zu der gewählten Antwort? In der richtigen Antwort stehen selten die gleichen Wörter wie im Text: Achte auf Synonyme, Umschreibungen, Gegensätze usw.

USE OF ENGLISH

2 **LANGUAGE** **A weekend in the woods** ____/ 13

Complete the text with the correct *emphatic/reflexive pronouns*.

I ______________ was never so wild about the idea of spending a weekend in the woods: Luisa ______________ was the one who suggested it. I let ______________ be talked into it by her. But I actually enjoyed ______________ more than she did!

Luisa's uncle finally brought ______________ to a phone and confirmed that we could use his cabin. He'd built it ______________ in the wilderness of Ontario.

When we got there, we saw that some animals had made ______________ a home in the bedroom. Luisa was really scared that they would come back, but I'm sure they ______________ were frightened to do that while we were there. I started to clean the room but Luisa excused ______________ , saying she was allergic to animals.

Luisa spent most of the weekend entertaining ______________ with her smartphone.

I ______________ set off for a long walk in the woods each morning. I taught ______________ canoeing, went hiking and kept ______________ busy with fishing and birdwatching.

3 **LANGUAGE** **Working at the rodeo** ____/ 9

The manager of the rodeo is talking to the new ticket takers. Complete her speech with the correct form of *have to*, *be allowed to* or *be able to*.

You ______________________________ *(arrive)* at work on time! If you are ill and ______________________________ *(not come)* to work, you ______________________________ *(let us know)* as soon as possible. Last year, ticket takers ______________________________ *(not wear)* a uniform; this year, you ______________________________ *(wear)* a uniform. The factory ______________________________ *(not finish)* the uniforms yet, so we ______________________________ *(not give)* them to you until next week. Starting next week, ticket takers ______________________________ *(buy)* two tickets each week at a lower price for their friends and family. You ______________________________ *(not choose)* the seats.

4 WORDS At a rodeo

____/8

a Complete these rodeo words.

____/7

1 a wild horse
2 a large round object horses sometimes jump over at rodeos
3 what a horse does when it jumps with two or four feet off the ground
4 an event in which people try to beat each other at sports, games etc.
5 a kind of hard hat you wear to protect your head
6 used to keep a helmet on your head or a saddle on a horse
7 a race in which riders on each team change places
8 what you sit on when you're riding a horse

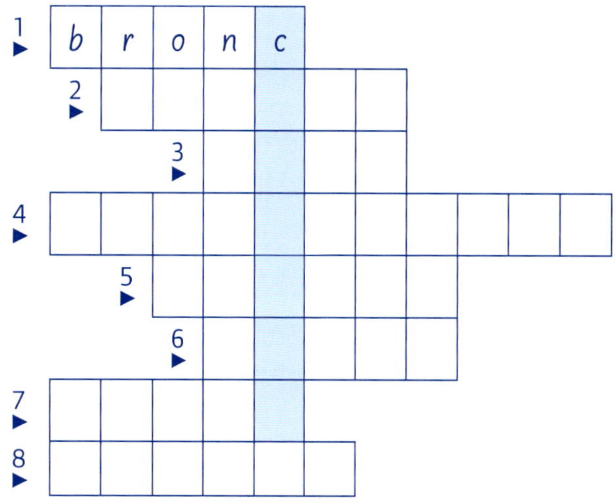

b Write the letters from the blue boxes to complete the following sentence.

____/1

Some people say that rodeos are a kind of ______________________________ to horses.

5 WORDS Going camping

____/11

What would you use these things for on a camping trip? Write down one idea for each thing: you do not have to write full sentences.

1 horn *to scare animals*
2 tent ______________________
3 backpack ______________________
4 gun ______________________
5 stick ______________________
6 food ______________________
7 trap ______________________
8 candle ______________________
9 sleeping bag ______________________
10 shovel ______________________
11 canoe ______________________
12 hatchet ______________________

6 MEDIATION Finding Anne of Green Gables on Prince Edward Island

___/9

Verwende die Informationen aus folgendem Text. Bearbeite die Aufgaben (1–5) stichpunktartig auf Deutsch. Es ist keine wörtliche Übersetzung nötig, die Aspekte müssen inhaltlich jedoch vollständig erfasst sein. Einzelwörter genügen nicht als Antwort.

Lucy Maud Montgomery published the first of eight stories about the red-haired Anne Shirley in 1908. Anne of Green Gables was a hit. The stories are set in the town of Avonlea in the Canadian province of Prince Edward Island. The name Avonlea was invented by Montgomery, but the town is very similar to Cavendish, where Montgomery grew up.

Over 50 million copies of Anne of Green Gables have been sold. Every year tourists from around the world bring millions of dollars to Prince Edward Island, the smallest Canadian province.

On the island, visitors can tour the house that was the model for Green Gables, where Anne comes to live at the age of 11. It was the home of Montgomery's cousins, a brother and sister who never married and who were the inspiration for Matthew and Marilla, who adopt[1] Anne. In the house, fans will recognize objects from the stories in each room. Trails lead to sites from the books such as the Haunted Wood and Lover's Lane. You can even take part in activities like making ice cream with Anne and other characters.

Serious fans will also want to visit the house where L. M. Montgomery was born in 1874, near the town of Cavendish. Objects that can be viewed there include a copy of Montgomery's wedding dress and scrapbooks of her life.

Cavendish is all about Anne. You can watch performances of two different Anne musicals, fill your bags with souvenirs such as Anne-style hats with red braids from the many souvenir shops, take a ride in a wagon pulled by horses like the one driven by Matthew in the books, and more. Several cafes sell foods and drinks enjoyed by Anne.

You don't have to pay to see one of the most important sights in the area: the beautiful landscapes of Prince Edward Island, which Montgomery lovingly describes in each of the Anne books.

[1] **(to) adopt** [ə'dɒpt] adoptieren

LERNTIPP

Zur Lösung dieser Aufgabe musst du keine ganzen Sätze schreiben. Achte aber darauf, dass deine Antworten dennoch vollständig sind. Bei manchen Aufgaben musst du weniger Aspekte eines Themas nennen, als im Text erwähnt werden.

1 Was hat die Kleinstadt Cavendish mit den Anne-Büchern zu tun?

____

____ (1 P)

2 Welche Verwandten (zusammen mit ihrem Haus) von Montgomery waren wichtig für die Entstehung der Bücher und warum (2 Aspekte)?

____

____

____ (2 P)

3 Was kann man beim „Green Gables"-Haus unternehmen (2 Aspekte)?

____

____

____ (2 P)

4 Was kann man in Cavendish machen (3 Aspekte)?

____

____

____ (3 P)

5 Welche Sehenswürdigkeit kann man kostenlos besichtigen?

____

____ (1 P)

7 GUIDED WRITING A special place

____ / 15

A friend of yours from Canada will be visiting you next week.
Write him/her an email describing

- a special place you want to take him/her in your town/city,
- what you can do there,
- the meaning of the place in your life.

Find a suitable beginning and ending.
Write about 150 words. Write the text in your exercise book.

8 SKILLS Ask an expert

____/11

Ask questions to find out more about Canada's ancient giant[1] beavers.

You: ____________________

____________________ (1 P)

Expert: The first of Canada's giant beavers, which were herbivores, lived about 30 million years ago.

You: ____________________ (1 P)

Expert: A herbivore is an animal that only eats plants.

You: ____________________

30 million years ago. *(Go back to the topic of when giant beavers lived.)* (1 P)

____________________ (1 P)

Expert: The last ones died about 10,000 years ago.

You: ____________________ (1 P)

Expert: We don't really know why they died. The climate changed then: maybe it wasn't the right climate for them.

You: ____________________

____________________ (1 P)

Expert: Well, at that time there were periods of warm weather and then periods of very cold weather. Not all animals survived that change. It also meant that some plants[2] didn't survive. Animals that ate those plants might have starved.

You: ____________________ (1 P)

Expert: They lived in lakes near swamps.

You: ____________________ (1 P)

Expert: The giant beavers were about two and a half metres long.

You: ____________________ *(Show interest.)* (1 P)

____________________ (1 P)

Expert: They were about one metre tall.

You: ____________________ (1 P)

Expert: They were about one metre tall.

[1]**giant** [ˈdʒaɪənt] Riesen- [2]**plant** [plɑːnt] Pflanze